I0815496

Still Here

Still Here

Life Together on the Long Way Home

MARY BETH CHAPMAN

STEVEN CURTIS CHAPMAN

with

Lawrence Kimbrough

PUBLISHING®
BRENTWOOD, TENNESSEE

Printed in China

979-8-3845-3373-3

Published by B&H Publishing Group
Brentwood, Tennessee

Author Representation: one:eight entertainment

Dewey Decimal Classification: 306.81
Subject Heading: MARRIAGE / CHRISTIAN
LIFE / DOMESTIC RELATIONS

Cover design by B&H Publishing Group.
Photography by Micah Kandros.

1 2 3 4 5 • 29 28 27 26

Dedication

From Mary Beth

"Not today, Zurg!" The fact that I'm writing this dedication for a book Steven and I wrote about our marriage means I get to use a *Toy Story* reference, where evil emperor Zurg is attempting to destroy the virtuous Buzz Lightyear. Buzz emphatically says to him, "Not today, Zurg!"—which is a term we've used a lot, whenever we've had large or small Chapman victories over the *real* enemy who's tried destroying us throughout our forty-one-plus years of marriage. He hasn't taken us out yet, nor will we let him! We make choices daily, and we walk forward hand in hand to continue pushing back the darkness, choosing each other, which is not easy when you are a sinner married to a sinner. But as of this writing? "NOT TODAY, ZURG!"

Steven, from the rain and the empty zoo on our honeymoon to standing at the crib of our firstborn granddaughter in Ireland, you have chosen me every day without fail and continue to do so. I know it's not easy because, well, I'm me! I'm complicated and I'm nothing like you, and I know for sure it wears thin on most days. But there you are, every day, every minute, choosing me. I love you and I choose you right back—now and for the rest of the time we have together. I can't believe I get to do this crazy-full, awe-filled, amazing life with you!

And, of course, I dedicate this book to the obvious: Emily, Tanner, Caleb, Julia, Will, Jillian, Shaoey, Stevey, Maria, Eiley, Della, Verity, Noble, Ollie, Faye, and Jack—so far, a party of eighteen! You all have seen Mom and Dad at their best and for sure have weathered us at our very worst. For all the times we had to sit you down and ask you to forgive us, to all the laughter we've shared, to the times when all our hearts have been broken into a million pieces, we are so grateful to the Lord for sustaining us, for holding us, and for allowing us to hobble together and watch all of you live your lives. You go! All of you! Go change the world!

From Steven

As you will soon learn, if you continue reading past our dedications (and I sure hope you will!), this book was something we weren't quite sure we would, or should, ever attempt. And as Mary Beth has alluded to in her beautiful dedication comments, there have been many reasons thrown at us by one very ruthless and yet very defeated enemy "to not to," as Mater from Disney's *Cars* would say. Lots of Disney movie references here. Not sure what that says about us, other than the fact that we've watched a lot of them, many times through the years! (We promise we will not be quoting only Disney characters in this book.)

So, where to begin with writing the dedications for it? I want to say thank you to so many people, far more than I could begin to list here, whom God has placed in our lives over the years to listen to us, pray for us, counsel us, cheer us on, impart wisdom, laugh with us, cry with us—*everyone* who has walked this journey with us and been woven into the fabric of our beautiful, messy story. I can only ask God to let you know who you are and how priceless your friendship has been to us. Without each of you, this book would certainly not have been written.

With that said, I dedicate it to the inner ring in our "circle of life" (no, not another Disney reference!)—Emily and Tanner, Caleb and Julia, Willy Frank and Jilly Jane, Shaoey, Stevey Joy, and Maria. Your love, support, patience, encouragement, forgiveness, and grace are inextricably woven into the story that this book tells. Thank you!

To the seven new chapters in our Chapman story who have brought us greater joy, laughter, and sweetness than we could've ever imagined—Eiley, Della, Verity, Noble, Ollie, Faye, and Jack. Thank you for giving us our favorite names and our best jobs ever as Grammy and PopPops!

And, of course, to my bride, the one who has walked every step beside me. Thank you for never giving up and never letting go of my hand and my heart. Thank you for being "still here" with me and being willing to wade into the murky, scary waters of sharing our story, in hopes that together we can encourage others on their own journey to know the goodness and faithfulness of our God. Wherever this journey takes us, I always find my home in your eyes.

Finally, to the One who has so faithfully loved and kept us, be all the honor, glory, and praise . . . now and forever!

Contents

Introduction

Keeping It Real

Well, we're still here. *Still Here.* Together.

And on some days, to be honest with you, we'd have a hard time explaining to you how that's happened, other than to simply say it's all and only by God's goodness and grace!

It sure hasn't come from doing everything right, we can tell you that. It also hasn't come from having everything easy. You know some of what we mean by that. There's just nothing simple, even about such a simple statement that says we're "still here." It's still a miracle. We know it.

And we're still working at it. Forty years in, and yet here's the truth. Something could easily pop up between us this afternoon, out of nowhere, and out might come, who knows?—a spark of anger, a sigh of frustration, an old insecurity, maybe another tired excuse about a disappointed expectation, something that just hits one or the other of us the wrong way, and we could be right back at it again, as if we hadn't learned anything in all this time.

Except to know we shouldn't dare write a book about it.

Much less, to write it *together*.

Seriously, what are we thinking here? We've both had a lot of different counselors and therapists over the years to help us better understand ourselves and our situation, and probably none of them would go along with this, knowing us as they do. Yet for some reason, we keep thinking the Lord is guiding us to go ahead. To write this book. Together! (Lord, have mercy.)

So here we go.

We'll start by saying thanks. Thanks to you. We've grown accustomed to not being surprised when you and others say they're interested in hearing how we're doing these days. We're truly grateful to know you care. We hope you know how much and how deeply we appreciate it. All the love. All the kind and supportive words. All the prayers. We've said publicly many times that we know it's your prayers—prayers from so many people like you—that have helped sustain us and carry us through to where we are now.

It's just that we're also accustomed, more than anyone else can be, to what everyday life is like for us here at our house. And we know what a challenge it's been, what a challenge it can still be sometimes, to keep the two of us not only on the same page but on the same bookshelf. Without winding up in the true crime section.

That's why we've always thought it'd be a whole lot easier, especially now that we're closer than ever to riding off into the sunset (whatever that actually means), if we could just go on fooling everybody into thinking we've got it completely figured out, that the Chapmans, man, are just these amazing people who have this amazing marriage and family. How in the world do they do it? If you could only be more like *them*!

Well, you probably are. More than you know. We're all a lot alike. That's one of life's most heavily guarded secrets, it seems, and it's one of the big misconceptions we want to help shatter with you during this time when we've got you to ourselves like this. There's a lot more "normal" than you realize to whatever bothers you or embarrasses you the most about yourself or about your life. Whether it's something that still knows how to find you and pick at you from your past, all noisy and threatening like, or something that continues to upset you so much about your present, none of it makes you weird or worse or a whole lot different from anybody else you might brush up against later in the day.

Even us. We hope you're already hearing that.

We could all benefit, we think—every one of us—from being more aware that most of our struggles are experienced to some degree by nearly everyone else. And yet, for some ridiculous reason, we almost universally work hard to cover them up. We yank down the blinds on who we really are, going to just about any length to prevent people from thinking something different about us than the illusion we want them to believe. The illusion we sometimes confuse for reality.

For example, when you're the couple who's known for a song like "I Will Be Here," and then you're "still here" forty years later, people might think you've figured out everything there is to know about marriage. Even if you clearly tell them differently.

When you're the parents of five grown kids, each one of them a well-adjusted, mature young adult, and they still seem to enjoy hanging out with their mom and dad on occasion, people can tend to think you've figured out everything there is to know about family and raising children.

When you've done the ten thousandth interview where you've been asked again how you're able to do it all—maintain an active career, manage all the tugs on your time and your schedule, keep advocating for children and families impacted by adoption, and, to top it all off, withstand the kind of heart-wrenching loss that a lot of wives, husbands, moms, dads, and families don't ever survive—people think you've obviously got a lot to say that the rest of us can learn from.

If people only knew.

We may *look* old and almost wise enough to be grandparents because, guess what? We ARE grandparents—Grammy and PopPops to seven beautiful grandkids at last count. But something's gone screwy for us on the way to reaching that point in life where we're supposed to be sage and stalwart and steady through the corners. We don't have it down the way we always expected to have it if we ever made it long enough to be grandparents ourselves. Most of what's kept us standing through all the things we've been through—plus all the things we've *put* each other through—has been just this stubborn determination that refuses to give up, even after a whole lot of mess-ups. It's been grace and repentance. Grace. And more repentance. Grace. And forgiveness. Grace. And God.

It's been God.

In other words, we may be the Steven Curtis and Mary Beth Chapmans. The people in the public eye. The couple you know because of these songs you've liked to sing along to, songs the Lord has continued to birth out of our cherished but challenging journey through the years. We hope they've been just as encouraging to you on yours. But the way we got here and the way we've stayed here has not come from putting together a perfect performance, or anything close to it, not from either one of us. There's really nothing special here, not in *us*.

Except that we're still here.

But being *Still Here* is something pretty special all its own.

Because, look, marriage can be hard. Parenting, hard. Doing your job again today without wanting to quit? On some days, hard. Life is just hard. Yet maybe the biggest achievement every day, when life and family get so unbearably hard, is not found in getting the answer you want, or the apology you want, or the relief you want so badly from whatever stress or struggle seems so insurmountable to you right now. In the likely event that everything doesn't clear up for you exactly how you hoped by tomorrow—in the likely event that you're still here in the hard in the morning—perhaps the winning is found most often just in doing the hard. By God's grace, by God's strength, *doing the hard.* And then doing it again. And wherever possible, doing it together.

It's what we've written this book to say.

We'd love to think, as we go along, you'll read something that registers with you and speaks directly to a situation you're facing in your life right now. That'd be wonderful. We'd love it if some of our stories and memories, including even the chicken-scratch parts that we're still sort of writing out and working through as we speak, might somehow twist around into something that sounds like helpful advice to you in real time. Or good advice about what *not* to do, *any* time! (We're actually better at giving that!)

But mainly, we decided to go ahead and write this book because we felt like God was telling us not to wait until we'd figured everything out. We'd be waiting a long time if we did . . . like, forever! The only thing we came to talk about with you is what's here and what's happened with us, and what we're hopefully still learning from what we've observed in the middle of it. No five easy steps to follow. No numbered points to jot down. No charts, graphs, and straightly drawn arrows. Just openness and honesty, mixed in with a lot of hard-fought humility, mainly because of all the opportunities God has found for humbling us. And because of how many ways we've fought it. And fought each other over it.

Our story is not as polished and put together as we wish. We're guessing yours is not either. Neither is theirs, most likely—the people who go around acting like it is. (God bless 'em if it is.) For the rest of us, not every day is one we're proud of, and not every wishful plan for the future falls together like a Hallmark Christmas movie. We can't in good conscience tell you how much better your life would be if you'd just do it like us. We're rarely at that place where we can just pull out a Bible verse to lace up nice and pretty around our problems.

We're simply inviting you to come over and let's talk about what's real. Real with us and real with you. And often really hard. Too real and too hard for any of us to think we could live it better by ourselves. Without each other.

Chapter 1

It's Crazy

Steve and Mary Beth, at sixty.

So much for young love.

And so much for sixty being the new forty. (It is not.) Sixty, we've found, is just straight-up sixty. Six-oh. If you're ninety, we're guessing it sounds long-ago young and nostalgic. If you're thirty, we remember it sounding faraway old and decrepit. But from where we sit at the moment, it just . . .

Sixty just sounds like *us* now.

And it's fine. We're good with that.

Fortunately, we got an early start at it. We've now spent about twice as many years looking out at life together as we did in the twentyish years growing up before we met. Every experience, every decision, every thought on the world, every discussion about matters both important and relatively unimportant. Even when we're alone, or when we're apart but still talking and thinking about any of these things, whether with friends or family or perfect strangers, we can't ever do it without factoring the other one into it. *What would HE think? What would SHE think?* He/she is always there, somewhere.

So it's the only way we know anymore. Viewing life together. Not that we still don't often look at things differently from each other. We do. (We really, *really* do.) Between our two sets of eyes are two drastically different sets of built-in temperaments. We have many different, mighty different takes on things. We'll tell you a lot more about some of that. Later.

But we're codependent enough by now—in all the right, good, and awful ways—that even when our clashes of perspective are the most severe, the most exasperating, there's still a weird sort of comfort and familiarity to it. We're not sure we could function without it. Even the parts of each other's personality that we don't particularly like—if those prickly pieces were suddenly not there, we have a feeling it would throw us off, despite how much we might've thought we wanted the change. Because then we'd be forced to learn a whole new playbook, and we've got so many years invested in this one already.

Now maybe that's not the best. Some people say you can lose yourself that way, by being so tied into another person's thoughts and moods and opinions. But we've been living inside each other's heads for so long—in our work and our family, our faith, our everything—it's not like we can just pull the rip cord on it and trust ourselves to find another way to the ground. Our life, the way we do it, has been happening like this for as long as we can remember.

Since 1984.

Want to go back with us for a second? To how we started? We've both told our life stories in print before, so there's a possibility you've heard this part of it twice. If not, or even if so, here's the two-minute version.

We met in college, at Anderson University, a small Christian school about an hour northeast of Indianapolis. Being such a compact little campus, it didn't take long to start spotting the same people on a regular basis, just in the normal rotation of walking to class or to lunch or whatever. You started recognizing names and faces pretty fast.

And yet the two of us first became acquainted through the mail. More specifically, through the mailbox. The school post office delivered student mail into a central hub of keyed mailboxes, arranged alphabetically by name, with two people assigned to each slot. (The threat of identity theft, obviously, was not a thing yet.) And since even then we so happened to share the same last name—both of us were already Chapmans from birth—that's how, in the clever story God was writing, we started receiving our mail at the same address before we'd even introduced ourselves.

Now neither of us would say we'd gone into that term at college feeling overly eager to find romance, much less to see ourselves getting into a serious relationship. Yet we seemed to have found our just-right person anyway, without intentionally looking. It started small and offhand, like most things do. But after a month or more of hinting and hanging around together, including the splurge of a Red Lobster outing for our first real dinner date—and our first kiss (and oh, what a kiss it was!)—we were already daring to imagine our future with the other one inside of it.

You could almost even set it to music.

I still remember the first time I felt the power of your kiss / it hit me like a bolt of lightning / I said I will never recover from this / and like the words from the mouth of a prophet / I have lived to see those words come true / just look at me now / I'm still reeling / with every little kiss

from "With Every Little Kiss"

By spring break, we'd put a ring on it. And by fall—October 13, 1984—we'd gotten married. We pulled away from the church parking lot in Springfield, Ohio, with fifty dollars in our pocket and a trusty green Ford Pinto as our sole means of transportation. A nineteen-year-old girl and her twenty-one-year-old husband, knowing love would keep them together.

It barely kept us together another day.

We followed up our wedding night (which was really . . . FUN! Can we say that in this book?) with maybe the least best option ever for a honeymoon destination—the Cincinnati Zoo on a cloudy, rainy Sunday. Not exactly the happiest place on earth. The foul weather left us feeling strangely sad and melancholy, which was kind of surprising, to say the least, for a pair of doe-eyed newlyweds. But a bad time at the zoo can do that to you. Even the animals in habitat knew it wasn't a good day for being outside wandering around, even if your new love interest was walking right beside you.

Soaked and heavyhearted, we drove off at closing time toward our first little cubbyhole in Nashville on our *second* night as husband and wife, wending our way through a sad, gloomy fog of silence and tears. And a creeping sense of fear. Had we made a terrible mistake in getting married? Had we let our love and feelings and the excitement of our wedding day obscure all the signs that said we were not the best fit for each other? Because this wasn't the way it was supposed to be. This didn't feel right at all. Should we be feeling so distant and different? Already?

Rolling down the highway, we were suddenly, and strangely, facing the harsh oncoming headlights of a new reality that didn't look nearly as bright as it had seemed only a few days earlier.

The kids started coming early too. Barely six months into our marriage, our new little puppy dog, Peso—continuing with the animal theme—ate a full blister pack of birth control pills that he had procured from Mary Beth's purse. As it turns out, missing just one of those little tiny pills can bring about some very big changes in your life! Though still only two young'uns ourselves, now we had a young'un of our own.

First came Emily, then Caleb, then when we least expected it, our next big surprise, Will Franklin—the two boys arriving only a year and a half apart. Not until much later did we round out the group with three more additions to the Chapman clan, each welcomed into our family from China through the miracle of adoption in the early 2000s: Shaohannah ("Shaoey"), Stevey Joy, and our precious Maria, who lives now with Jesus.

So there you have it—some of the top-forty highlights from the last forty jam-packed years, captured in a very small nutshell.

Which brings us now to sixty.

It's not like we didn't see sixty coming. We could do the math. We could follow the trends. The newspaper may be a dying medium of communication but not because they started running out of fresh material for the obituary page every morning. Getting older is what we humans do. It wasn't something God was going to let the two of us have a pass on just because we'd been such kids when we started or because we still felt like kids so much of the time, even as grownups.

So it's not the *fact* that it's happened—going from zero to sixty—but the *way* it's happened that's been the surprise. Whatever we thought was coming down the pike when we left the zoo on that day after the wedding, we had no idea the crazy we were driving into.

And we don't necessarily mean "crazy" as a compliment.

Most of us think we're going to be the exception. Most of us, when we look ahead into adulthood, think we're going to succeed where others have failed. We're going to know what to do where others have perhaps lost their way and lost their minds. And lost their families. We're going to make the kinds of plans and decisions, we're going to build the kind of home and marriage and personal character traits that'll help us handle whatever comes. We'll do it together and we'll do it better. Better than everybody else. We'll face every challenge with a cool head, with the right answers, with style and with grace. People will respect us for that. Our spouse will love us for that. We'll always be on the same page. And when we're not, we'll talk it out and pray it over until we can get there, until we can both feel good about it. Then when we're old and the kids have grown up, we'll have the whole family all together for Thanksgiving—this year and every year and for all the years that Thanksgivings are there to be had. And everything's going to be the way it should be. Because why shouldn't it be, if we do life the way we know we can do it? If we do it the right way.

That's what we think. Or at least that's what we hope. Even the most pessimistic among us can't avoid feeling a little bit of a brush with this youthful brand of optimism. One of the people in our marriage knows pessimism personally (she'd rather call it *realism*). But even people like that, starting out, are pretty sure they've learned all the primitive skills necessary to protect themselves from being taken advantage of by life, from losing the ground they've worked so hard to recapture, from being caught blindsided when the other shoes start dropping. It's not going to happen on *their* watch, they can tell you *that*.

And yet none of us is ever quite ready for the crazy.

Parents know this when they see their own kids try to do it, to do a better job at adulthood than all the people who've come before them. We've lain awake at night thinking about them—at twenty, at thirty, out where they think they know everything. Young and smart. The bold and the beautiful. But they're not ready, any more than *we* were ready, any more than *our* parents thought we were ready, at twenty and thirty, ready for every contingency that could come along.

The good. The bad.

The very, very, very bad.

You don't get ready for that. You can't anticipate that. Not all of it. You just don't know the crazy you've signed up for until you're out there in the middle of it. And by then, you can only look up—like at sixty, like we're doing now—and wonder how you got here. And wonder how you're *still* here, apart from God just doing what He does, being so much bigger and better than all the big-talking stuff you thought you were bringing to this party. At least that's how it's been with us. It's been crazy.

That's the word we use a lot to talk about ourselves and our journey, this incredible ride we've been on for all these years and are still riding out today. Crazy exciting, crazy frightening. Crazy joyful, crazy hard. Crazy with blessings—like, super crazy with blessings—yet crazy also with stuff that has often seemed the polar opposite of blessings. We've had the kind of happy and surprising crazy you can only believe if you look at it with a sideways wink and a smile, but also the kind of crazy that comes in screaming hot with a whole bunch of anger and illogical arguing. There's been the crazy that comes looking for us, and there's been the crazy we bring home and make everybody crazy ourselves. (Just know, the other person who's writing this book can be a whole lot of crazy sometimes. Don't tell him or her I said that.)

In all honesty, one reason we've shied away from writing all this crazy stuff is because of how disappointing we feared it might be for you to read some of it, perhaps to be disillusioned by it. Our life is not set to the tune of a love song on auto-repeat, although one of us has sung a certain love song about 100,000 times by now. We're not saying we're a total mess either. We can be a whole lot of crazy fun as well. Especially the girl one of us. But honestly—

Okay, we can be a total mess, that's true. We sort of *aren't*, but then again, we sort of *are*. Sometimes we *really* are.

But if God will get the glory, then we hope you don't mind hearing about our crazy life this way. Maybe, in fact, this is exactly what you've been needing somebody like us to say. That we can all be a crazy mess today and, by the abundant grace of

God, can still be only a sunrise away from another whole new beginning. It's true. Not just for us but for you too.

If that's what you want and need, you're welcome here. And you're welcome to keep coming along with us as we talk it through. Just don't expect to find us telling you The Chapman Way of Living Well—because, for one thing, we probably couldn't say it and keep a straight face. Of course, it's not that we haven't tried, prayed, pleaded, read the books, attended the conferences, and visited every counselor who would agree to see us in an attempt to do it as well as possible. If you've read the lyrics from many of these songs over the years, you've definitely heard the references of our deep desire and determination. Still, with all our endeavors and efforts over time to live well, we have found ourselves becoming more comfortable with being known as those who "*hobble well.*"

That's a phrase our son Caleb once wrote about us, trying to describe us to somebody else. To be clear, neither he nor any of the rest of our kids are under any illusion that their parents do or have always done everything well. No way. They've definitely seen us at our most "un-well-est," the times when every one of them, even when they were much younger people, were probably acting more maturely in the moment than their mom and dad. There have been plenty of times the two of us have looked at each other, evaluating the current condition of our marriage, our hearts, and our history, and the word *well* has not always been the first descriptor that pops into our minds.

But our son being able to say we've "hobbled well" is just maybe one of the most encouraging things that could be said of us. We've certainly done a lot of hobbling, the two of us. Life has hobbled us, as surely as it's hobbled you.

Now maybe if we'd done things better, and consistently treated each other better, and prayed better, and done our morning devotions better, hobbling wouldn't be our most applicable form of address. We're not suggesting "hobbling" should be the grand prize everybody is hoping to win when they reach for the big grab bag of life. Here's all we're saying: When the crazy comes and really starts flying, we've found it's better to hobble on together, hand in hand, than to head off in different directions. Better to waver and wobble alongside each other, one day at a time, than to wander away from this weird but sometimes wonderful person we walked in with.

Everyone stands to lose things, important things, when they give up on each other—things they may not ever get back. But of all the things we've done unwell in life and in marriage—and, sadly, there's a big book-length volume of them to choose from—the grace of God that's kept us together is the one trophy in this house that means the most to us.

It's really not a lot of fun, this hobbling. But compared to the option of falling totally apart, of going totally on our own, it's crazy not to do it.

We will dance / when the sun is shining / in the pouring rain / we'll spin and we'll sway / and we will dance / when the gentle breeze becomes a hurricane / the music will play / and I'll take your hand / and hold you close to me / and we will dance

from "We Will Dance"

When we finished our first two books, we were still in the early stages of the grief and trauma from losing Maria. It was hard to write all that. It was probably still too fresh for us to be emotionally ready for what telling that story would do to us.

But we were starting to be able to believe, by faith—and to a small degree, by sight—the truth of God and His Word that promises "Beauty Will Rise," even from the rock-hard soil of suffering and grief. Though we were still in the preliminary stages of it, He was preparing our broken hearts to accept a new world order, trusting His sovereignty, goodness, and great love, and choosing to believe that even our family's torturous undoing could somehow be part of a "Glorious Unfolding" story.

Among the most telling visuals that spoke to this beautifully glorious outcome was Maria's Big House of Hope, a magnificent six-story medical care center in Luoyang, China—part of the passionate work of the hard-loving team and supporters at Show Hope, the nonprofit we founded with a mission of caring for orphans by engaging the church and reducing barriers to adoption.

This sky-blue structure, punctuated with fluffy painted clouds, was a bright spot among the mostly drab, gray buildings lining the streets of Henan Province. Truly a thing of beauty, and truly from the ashes. Home to excellent, holistic, and life-changing care for medically fragile orphans. Our hearts had barely felt like beating when we'd cut the ribbon on it in July 2009. The pain was still too fresh. We wanted Maria, way more than we wanted this, as beautiful as *this* was. But we quickly fell more and more in love with it—mostly because of how deeply we still loved her but also because of the tremendous efforts the caregivers there were providing. What an incredible difference they were making in so many lives. The Lord in His kindness was inviting us to celebrate Maria's legacy in a way that forever impacted and benefitted the lives of thousands of children who were brought inside those doors to be cared for, held, and loved, to be treated with holistic skill and, most important, with holy dignity.

But in 2019, we lost even that.

We won't go into what led our board and ourselves to arrive at the decision of shifting our focus elsewhere, but factors arose beyond our control that made staying there unworkable. We were left with no other real choice. We had to leave. Leave behind the beautiful blue building that bore our daughter's name and her delightful artwork throughout. Yes, leave it—knowing we'd likely never be back, that we'd probably never see it again. It hurts to this day.

It was a twist-your-gut kind of call to make. Really hard. It made for long cries and painful goodbyes. Serious discussions followed by sleepless nights. It was the only right thing to do. We knew it. But we did not—did NOT—want to do it.

In the end, looking back on it, the almost immediate arrival of the COVID scare made the wisdom of our corporate decision seem providential in retrospect. But at the time, in the sharp teeth of it—along with our daughter Emily, who was just then stepping up into the role of Show Hope's executive director—all we felt were pain and loss. A new churning of grief.

It was horrible. Another season of our lives where nothing made any sense. None of it.

But the stress and discomfort of it took us back to a place where, at one point in our lives, another major decision had been staring us in the eye, waiting to be made—another decision, like this one, that didn't make a whole lot of sense either.

Back in the late nineties, when we first began feeling the stirring in our heart to consider growing our family through adoption, our tendency was to view it through the lens of what seemed most sensible and reasonable. Were we not busy enough already? Wearing ourselves thin, doing the "ministry" we'd already been entrusted with? We'd pretty much figured out how to do the three-kid thing by then, even with Dad on the road half the time. Our family was working about as well as it could work. We didn't see how we could possibly add one thing more.

Yet after a lot of prayer and some pretty undeniable nudges from the Lord—many of them disguised as some not-so-subtle nudges from Emily!—we'd done it. And in the process of doing it, He made Himself real to us in ways we had never experienced before.

There's nowhere in the world we've ever felt closer to Him—ever!—than in Changsha, China, the day we were handed our daughter Shaoey for the first time. The moment this tiny, beautiful treasure was placed in our arms, it was as if God whispered to our hearts more clearly than either of us had ever experienced, to say, "This is as close as you'll ever come to understanding My grace and My love for you." God was giving us a glimpse of His heart for us in a way that would change us forever.

And had it not been for that—and for all the crazy life occurrences that came after that, including the joy of getting to know and to parent our Stevey Joy and our Maria—we'd never have been in Louyang to begin with, where Maria's Big House of Hope was located. We wouldn't have felt forced to *part* with a project so precious to us, but we also wouldn't have been able to *partner* with it for as long as we did.

So, while it hurt to see such a significant chapter of our lives come to a close, we are so very grateful for the years we invested and the relationships we made. They will always be some of the most indisputable evidences of God at work that we've ever witnessed. We got to see—to SEE for ourselves—"the LORD's goodness in the land of the living" (Ps. 27:13). And who knows? In His time, He might one day open the door again for us to walk right back into some of those same places, maybe down the same hallways where we once got to meet and visit and care for young kids who had nowhere else to go.

But even if we don't, and even though it hurts, we've seen the goodness of God there.

And when you think about it, that should be all we need. We don't need to understand why things happened or why He allowed us to go through it or why His goodness so often comes bundled inside so much badness. We just need to know He's here. We just need to know He's good.

And be crazy enough to believe it.

So that's some of what we've been doing since we sat down and wrote a book last.

We've been adding up grandbabies, long enough that some of them aren't babies anymore: Eiley, Della, Verity, Noble, Olive, Faye, and Jack.

Our younger girls—Shaoey and Stevey Joy—have each grown up, gone to college, and stepped out into the wild blue yonder of young adulthood. We've seen in them, like in all our kids—like with Emily, our resident theologian and deep thinker—certain traits and trajectories that we wish we had. She says things to us sometimes that make us think, okay, she's doing life a generation better than us. And that's awesome, when you see it and hear it in your kids. We've studied enough about family histories and ancestry to appreciate the value of breaking chains and moving forward. And we love those times—not all the time, but thankfully now a lot of the time—when we can see in them, in all the kids, how they're moving the needle forward. Or at least finding their way and figuring it out.

Caleb and Will have been making music—great music, some of the best music we've ever heard. In fact, we're convinced their band, Colony House, is the best rock band on the planet! But, yes, it's *rock* music, which is outside the category we're most familiar with, even though their music is still very much woven together with the threads of their faith. They're beautiful souls, these two guys of ours, willing to ask questions in their songwriting that most people, when *we* were their age, were too polite to mention. Too afraid or repressed or whatever. But it's a different and much harder world they've grown up in and are living in. And, of course, they've lived through things individually that don't lend themselves to settling for easy answers.

So the music goes on. Because the music, for us, has always been more than just generic songs about generic situations. It's always been a way of processing our life, wrestling with our own journey. We can trace through the whole catalog of Steven Curtis Chapman music, and it's like we're right back there again, chronicling where we were, what we were doing, how we were trying to understand or handle some of the distinct struggles and challenges we were facing at the time. Our marriage and family are woven into the fabric of those songs. All the music is born out of lived experience.

Steven: A great example of this is the creative season that came during COVID for me. I honestly wasn't sure if I would make another album again, given the ways the music business had changed so much, with streaming and everything, and with how differently people consume and engage with music these days. Do artists even make whole albums anymore? And even if they do, I was struggling with another question that, ridiculous as it sounds, was a very real struggle for me: Did the world need another Steven Curtis Chapman album? Or even another Steven Curtis Chapman song for that matter? (This is some of the silly yet serious stuff that we insecure, brooding artists find ourselves ruminating over. See, I like to bring others into the struggle with me so that I feel less insecure!)

But during COVID, I began to find myself having song ideas that I felt compelled to write, some things I felt like I wanted and needed to say. There was so much uncertainty and loss all around us. The music business, like just about every other business, was effectively shut down, so lots of questions were swirling around with that. On top of it, we were personally trying to process two devastating losses: one, a dear friend, and another, a precious family member.

Ideas of things I wanted to say were beginning to flow, but as I began to try to form them into songs, the naysayers in my head began to whisper. I found myself wondering if I even knew how to write songs anymore. Or if I'd *ever* known how to write them. Maybe it was all a fluke. Or maybe God had just given me the gift to write those songs for a season, but now the gift had departed. Okay, I know that sounds crazy, but I was really battling it out in my head.

Mary Beth: Yes, you've only written something like twenty-four records. (Cue the eye roll.)

Steven: I know! I'm just trying to be honest here. It's kind of embarrassing to even say it out loud, but as my trash can was getting full of wadded-up pieces of paper, my head and heart were getting full of frustration and fear.

And on top of it all was the nagging question of, not just whether I *could* do it but whether I *should* do it, because every album and new creative chapter brings with it plenty of angst and struggle on the home front. Mary Beth has lived a life of having to endure me drifting off into the faraway land of writing and recording an album. She's endured it patiently (most of the time), but she's also been quick to let me know that it ain't easy.

Mary Beth: I knew he had more songs in him. I knew he had things he needed to say, and I wanted him to say them. I really did. I fight my own battles of knowing this is what he's supposed to do with the gifts God has given him but also feeling the weariness of it, the loneliness and the longing for a simpler and quieter life, especially at this phase of our marriage and life together. So, yes, I was having a lot of those "here we go again" feelings rising up.

Steven: Yeah, it was scary that way too, because—she's right, she means what she says. She is truly my biggest fan and cheerleader. That's not just stage talk. None of what I've done in this career would have happened without her being right beside me every step of the way, giving her support and encouragement. And her honesty. It's the truth. And yet this creative-musician life of mine is a two-edged sword. It's part of why she loves me, I think, but it's also part of what drives her up the wall with me. Could and should I really do this to her again? Get back up on this treadmill? The days and nights in the studio? Another promotional tour? And then all the meetings and interviews and radio singles and the tour dates that follow? No matter how hard I may try to manage it and balance it, there's still a toll that it takes on her. There's the tension it creates, and everything that comes with it.

Somewhere in the process of all this, I ended up on the floor in my studio one day. I would like to say I was praying, which I was. But it felt more like a full-on wrestling match with God, pouring my heart out, trying to figure out what to do and what not to do with all the fear and confusion and questions and struggles I was carrying. I was literally pounding the floor as the tears flowed, and finally I decided to just start writing/singing exactly what I was experiencing in the moment. It was a moment of surrender that led to what would become the album called *STILL*. And every time I sing or listen to those songs again, they "still" take me back to those days, and those times, and to all the things I was feeling.

I've been thinkin' and thinkin' / 'til I just don't know what to think anymore / I've been trying to figure it all out / poundin' my fist on the floor / but I'm not givin' in to this fear and this pain / these tears in my eyes means there's blood in my veins

I'm alive / I wanna taste every tear that falls / I wanna face every fear that calls my name / I'm gonna stand and say I'm alive / I wanna take every breath God gives / like it's the precious gift that it is / I wanna live with every heartbeat reminding me / I'm alive

from "I'm Alive"

And here's where that leaves us today. Very much alive. Struggling and sad on some days. Feeling really hopeful, happy, and excited about life on other days. And then there's all the rest of the days, where we're sort of fumbling around somewhere in between.

Sometimes it feels weird. Being sixty. Being home on the empty nest. It's also busy, just like your own life is busy. As busy as before, maybe even *busier* in certain ways, but without having the same kind of bounce to it, or at least the same kind of ability to bounce back from it. Even the anniversary cards look old now, all lacy and gold foil—the kind we gave our grandparents back in the day. But we don't look *that* old . . . do we? (This is where you shake your head and say, "No, definitely not!")

But our life has been a wild one, no doubt. Some of it's been like a dream. The commercial success has certainly been beyond anything we ever imagined. It's provided us opportunities to experience a life full of so many amazing things. But success also brings along with it a whole lot of invisible baggage that you find yourself unpacking over time. We find it funny, for example, at sixty, having all these Doves and Grammys and gold-colored albums on the studio wall—all this crazy collection of goodness all around us—how often we're here in this house, just sitting here, all super quiet, so all alone.

You wouldn't think it, would you? Surely we've got a million other things we could be doing. And we do. Surely we could call anybody we want tonight and ask if they'd like to get together for dinner. Perhaps that's semi-true. But pretty rarely is our life a walk on the square on a summer night with a knot of good friends and a dish of yummy ice cream. Sometimes it's just lonely, just us, wondering if we ever come to mind when people think of inviting friends to be in their small group at church.

But otherwise, we're pretty normal, we think. We still fuss over little nothings when we'd be better off just letting them go—although, to be fair, we don't give nearly as loud a voice to it as we once did, which was a lot. We've found it's more fun now being proven silently right than trying to loudly argue our case for it. We can also escape into television binges when we should probably be doing something more productive, more important, more conducive to being a "good Christian." Which we still often do, of course. But we do get tired a lot. We tap out. We tempt easily into stuff like that.

See, we're all more alike than we let on.

Probably the biggest thing, though, more than all the other things, more than all the other topics of conversation that can heat up in our life, is the fact that one of us (guess which one) is hoping we could finally be close to being ready to start slowing down a little bit? Maybe? And yet the other one can't seem to stop running like a squirrel in all directions, unable to turn off whatever motor is supplying the energy for all that. The story of our life, so much of it, has felt like that. It's still like that. Stirred up and unsettled like that.

But . . .

We're still here.

And you'd be surprised how often that's what people tell us they think about the most when they think of us. Like, whenever we post a picture of ourselves or of our family doing something, even if it's nothing particularly special, just something wholly ordinary, they don't make many comments about the fifty number one songs. Or the concerts. Or the radio hits. Sure, there have been and continue to be so many stories, from so many folks who've journeyed with us, about how much the lyrics of a certain song or a certain album have connected with their lives and encouraged them on their own journey. And we are truly grateful for every one of those stories. But what we love most is people telling us, when they think of the Chapmans, they mostly just think of how they feel seeing us still together. Still here.

Because isn't that what really matters? We realize not everyone is able to tell that story. We realize, too, that we wouldn't be telling it either if not for so much grace and so many second and third and fifty million chances at trying to get ourselves back to where we could speak to each other in our inside voices, and then just choosing to keep after it . . . again.

The truth is, though, no matter where we're finding you today, there's still a legacy of commitment to God and commitment to each other that is still yours to grasp and go forward with—starting *now*, even if it didn't start before. Because life is hard for you too. You've been battling it out too. You've been struggling through the wars in your own life too. And you need to believe you can still hang in there too, in spite of all the times (like us) when maybe you didn't do what you were supposed to do.

Well, now you can. And now you *will.* And by the grace of God, we'll be doing it too, right along with you. Just *being* here. Just showing up and staying here.

Let's do it together.

The reason we're still here at sixty is not because we're better than others. We're still here at sixty because we've seen the worth of it in others, because of the "still here" encouragement and example of So Many Others. And though we hope we still have a way to go—and, for sure, we still have a lot to learn—we plan on being here the whole way through. To still be standing when the music stops. And we'd love knowing you're somewhere doing the same thing. Same as us. Burning the same light for other people to see and to keep heading toward.

Sixty is not the new forty.

Sixty is the new forever.

Love and learn / that's what we will do / love and learn / through the flood and through the flame / this world will turn / and the seasons will change / but there's nothing we can't get through / as long as we both hold onto the hand of God and each other / and take a lifetime / to love and learn

from "Love and Learn"

Chapter 2

It's Complicated

You might think, given the dramatically crazy ups and downs of our life, that the question we've asked the most often of God and of each other through the years is "Why?"

And to be clear, we've definitely asked "Why?" many times on this wild journey we've been on. We've wondered, for example, why so many amazing things have happened to a hillbilly kid from Kentucky and a simple midwestern girl from Ohio, things that have given us opportunities to be part of more incredible experiences than we can even count or remember. But for the most part, whenever we've asked "Why?"—when we've spoken it, thought it, whispered it, or even screamed it—it's come from a place of deep brokenness, pain, and inadequacy.

We recall being first-time parents, entering that season when our daughter Emily began to pelt us with it—"Why?"—that terrifying one-word question every parent grows to fear. Once you get to know us better, you'll see why hearing her ask us that question (and later, hearing all the other kids ask it, too) struck at such a sensitive place inside us because it exposed us as people who didn't always have the answers. And we hated that. Because isn't having the answers, the right answers, what good parents are supposed to do? Should there ever have been a little-kid question that we didn't have a big-person explanation for? And if we didn't, if we couldn't answer it, something must really be wrong with us. The "why" questions, to tell you the truth, can still make us feel a little bit that way today.

Thinking back, it was at about this time, dealing with those kinds of feelings as young struggling parents, when lyrics like these came pouring out:

Lord, if I could sit with You / at Your feet for an hour or two / I'm sure I'd ask too many questions / 'cause there's so much going on down here / that I must confess I just don't understand

from "Higher Ways"

So there have certainly been times—including the much darker and more difficult times—when we've wrestled desperately with wanting to know why. Like, why would such a terrible, traumatic thing happen to us, losing our daughter Maria? Not that anyone should ever have to go through an experience like that, but why *us*? We'd worked so hard at helping bring children and families together; we'd even opened our own home and hearts to adoption. "So, Lord, why would this be the way the story unfolds for *our* family?" Just being honest here. Thoughts like these could creep in sometimes.

And yet for the two of us, and really for our family as a whole, we've set aside most of the why questions—even though they can still hide out, waiting to strike. And they have often sneaked back in on us, on plenty of occasions. But the questions that have become bigger for us today (and are just about as difficult to answer) are the *how* questions.

How?

How do we do this? This marriage? This schedule? Even this day? The nonstop challenge of living this complicated life of ours. Both the expected and the unexpected. How do we navigate it? How do we manage it in a way that makes it even remotely manageable?

Do you feel the same thing sometimes yourself? The crunch of the schedule? The give-and-take where something's gotta give or we're all gonna tank? How do a man and a woman merge the different gifts and expectations we each bring into this relationship and somehow fuse them into one? Without starting a fire? Or without starting a fight? Because we've had enough fights around here for . . . shoot, maybe four or five marriages and lifetimes already.

Our marriage shouldn't work. A lot of times it *doesn't* work. But it's not from lack of trying. Especially with the calendar part of it. Hate to keep bringing it up, but that's our biggest pain point—the questions about what we need to be doing or to be focused on today (or this week, or this month, or this year), the things that'll get us where we're each trying to go, to what we're each trying to feel. To feel good about. Good about ourselves, good about the future.

We have wrestled it every way you can wrestle it, down to the ground and back again, with a lot of help from a lot of people, through all the various stages and dynamics of our family over a whole lot of years. And it just doesn't sync up. It's too complicated.

In the early and middle years, in the truly crazy years, a lot of the wrestling we did was over decisions we needed to make about travel and touring and all the tornadoes that spin around the life of a recording artist. When it came time for planning a new concert season, for example, was it better just to block off a whole set of dates? Go out and tour solid for one long uninterrupted run? Then be back home when all of it was over? Of course, being home was still consumed with writing and recording another album the next year, shoehorned around all the other stuff that our family and kids were doing, and everything else. Or was it better to try staggering it? Balancing it? Four days out, three days home. Something like that. Divvied up over a longer cycle of time.

We tried every configuration we could come up with. And all of them made for some great concerts. (Maybe you were there. Were you? Once or twice?) But none of those scheduling options was exactly awesome at accommodating what each of us wanted or needed during those phases of life. We struggled and strained not to go to war over it. Every year, every season, another new wrinkle would come up, requiring a snap decision to be made or some other recalculation. It gave us a lot of opportunities for turning against each other.

Even now, it's still an issue. We still battle with it.

We've tried graphing it out on paper, how to do it, how to combine our often-competing inputs and priorities into a single grid, then flow them out into a functioning calendar. Make them fit, make them behave. Make our life together a little more life and a lot more together.

And though we've each given ground in a lot of different areas trying to make it simpler than it's always been, there just seems to be no way. The days still show up with only twenty-four hours to offer. And when we get to talking and fussing and complaining about what we each need or want to happen inside all those days and hours . . .

It's just not happening.

Now maybe your most perplexing issues are something else entirely. Maybe the things that are really complicating your life right now involve—oh, let's say, handling a sickness, or caring for a loved one, or wrangling your kids, or keeping a business going. It could be so many things.

Or maybe the things you find yourself warring against the most often are the competing, overlapping voices that just never stop talking inside your own head. We all know how gnarly, knotty, and complicated *that* can be. There's one of us in particular who, even if the whole day has gone by without a single conversation with another human being, there's an exhaustion that settles in at night because—why?—because you've been talking to your own self all day! Maybe that's you too.

Maybe some days you feel like you're constantly struggling to quiet a stubborn temptation, or to weigh the pros and cons of a difficult decision, or to relitigate an old offense, perhaps relive a missed opportunity, or try to make sense of a disagreement you're having with somebody—like with this perplexing spouse of yours who is just not cooperating right now!

But marriage is only *one* way to experience it. All family relationships, even extended family relationships, invite a measure of complication that can be irritating at best, insurmountable at worst. Life just does it to us. There's so much to deal with and think about. So many things we're supposed to know and say. So many options to wade through and worry about. So much going on in the world, plus all the work-and-life balances that we never seem able to reconcile. So many emotional land mines to avoid. So many digs and jabs that could be thought but not spoken. Or, worse, could be spoken without thinking.

Man, we can be complicated people. And, man, life is complicated all around us. Whatever the various equations and frustrations that are conspiring to complicate your life right now—they are different enough to be your own, but they are the same enough to create a common language between us.

So in one way or another, you're probably like us in this. We keep thinking surely two relatively sane people can sit down and force even our most complicated things into alignment—because we truly do love each other, and we're committed to each other's happiness and well-being. But nearly every time we do it, every time we try to put together a plan for the summer, say, or for whatever season is coming up next, all we get when we're done are all these arrows flying, everywhere, in every direction. With nowhere to hang them all. No way to get our arms around them. And nothing at the bottom of the page that you can honestly call a solution to this impossible-sounding math problem of ours.

How can this be?

And *what* can we do about it?

You got any answers for us?

Because *answers* are what we've always been looking for. We are *answer* people. We like doing things right. It's hard to imagine any other couple where both the husband and the wife are more determined than us to come down on the side of not just what's best but what's *right.* We want to *be* right. We want others to *think* we're right. Getting it right is really important to us.

The only problem there—the part we have the hardest time with—is that we so often can't come together on what the right answer is.

So, what do you think we've done when we've found ourselves at these kinds of impasses—when the right thing isn't obvious, or at least isn't a consensus? We've read books, we've signed up for seminars, we've sat across from counselors who we wished would just come out and tell us what to do. Just give us the right answers to follow. Will you, please? Because right answers are everything. Right?

Well, that's a good question. Most of us think we live in a world where the difference between success and failure is found in having the right answers, in having the book that has the answer key in the back. In getting the answers right.

Why do some couples have such smooth, loving marriages? Because they've gotten the answers right.

Why do some parents have amazingly compliant kids? Because they've gotten the answers right.

Why do some people have a happier, more fulfilling, less chaotic and less challenging life than the rest of us do? Because when faced with the questions that come to all of us at one time or another, they chose the right answer, and they knew where to pop it in. They knew what to do.

And so, why do some marriages, the best marriages, seem to run on a calendar, on a schedule, on a shared set of desires and priorities, that appears to be working well for both of them? Because, obviously, these people are privy to answers that we mere pretenders simply are not.

That's what life tells us to believe.

Okay. So why didn't God, when He was writing the Bible, just give us a long list of right answers to follow, matched up to every human question? Why isn't the Scripture a series of life hacks and conditional formulas that we can personalize with our own data sets and then spit out practical step-by-step approaches to our most aggravating complications? What did He know that we didn't know when He decided not to communicate with us in a question-and-answer, rule-book format?

He must have known we needed something else a whole lot more.

More than we need answers.

Well, You know it's not the first time / and it will not be the last / when You find me here on my knees / praying for the storm to pass / but what I am really needing is much more than just relief / I am crying out for wisdom only You can give to me

from "How Do I Love Her"

Answers are good. Answers help.

But what we need is *wisdom*. What we need is *truth*. Wisdom and truth, more than answers and strategies, are what help us discover *how* to manage through the complicated.

In marriage. In parenting. In everything.

One of the classic examples from our life that was a huge get-the-answer-right category for us, especially when the first three of our kids were growing up, was deciding how much media we were willing to let them consume.

Basically, we're talking just movies and TV shows. That's pretty much all the content that was available at the time. And music too. But between concern for our young children's eyes and ears and hearts and minds, and the assault of new choices available to us in the Blockbuster video store era of entertainment, we felt the burden of drawing tight boundaries. And we were the type of parents who chose to restrict it pretty significantly. Who needed to be watching the Smurfs anyway? Or listening to the latest New Kids on the Block CD?

So we clamped down hard on it. Not only did we put a lot of limitation on what kinds of things the kids could watch; we even bought one of those censoring devices—a cuss box—that bleeped out bad language and replaced it with less offensive words, like "crud" or something. The speaker's voice would go mute, and the cleaned-up sentences would simultaneously appear in the form of a caption at the bottom of the screen. It was cutting-edge technology for careful twentieth-century families.

But wait, that's not all. The cuss box was merely *one* of the weapons we deployed in our tactics of cultural warfare. We even figured out a way to edit our own movies so that not even the presence of a PG-plus-rated scene in a film could spoil our viewing options. By pairing the "record" button on a camcorder with the "play" button on a VCR, we learned how to splice and dice the full-length feature from a videocassette until—voila!—we'd kept the gist of the movie together but, now stripped of unsightly material, we could actually *watch* it together. It felt like quite the little triumph. We'd faced the challenge of how to maneuver through the complicated world of media exposure, and we felt like we'd "kicked its tail." (That would be the cuss-box version.)

Now was there anything wrong with what we did? We don't think so. We'd taken a cautious, conservative stance on what we allowed to play through our children's heads, and we'd decided as parents that we were committed to going down that road. (This was also one of those early decisions in parenting that started earning Dad the family nickname of "Safety Steve.")

The only problem with parenting by the right-answer method is that you can get heavy on rules and then easily go light on communicating the *wisdom* behind them. You can shield everybody for the time being, for as long as you've got them under your roof or your control, but you can forget how one of the real tasks of parenting is to convey *truth* that prepares them for a lifetime of responding wisely themselves to new circumstances when you're nowhere around.

Rules are definitely part of the process—from protecting their minds to minding their manners—but nurturing your kids' relationship with you and with their heavenly Father is the part that eventually hangs around long enough to walk with them into the future. To borrow a great quote from Josh McDowell that we picked up somewhere early in our parenting, either from a conference or a book or something, which became sort of a wisdom mantra for us: "Rules without relationship leads to rebellion."

So one thing we tried to do, and probably overdid at times, was to try explaining to our young'uns the reasons for our restrictions, even if what they actually heard was more like the voice of the schoolteacher on Peanuts: "mwah wah wah, wah wah wah." It seemed important, even if it didn't make much sense to them at the time (a lot of the time), to work at growing our relationship with them, even as we were defining and enforcing the rules. We'd like to think the fruit of the relationships we have now with our kids is somewhat a result of some of those seeds that were planted back in those conversations. Answers have a job, yes, but answers can't do all the work for you.

This became even more clear to us as we raised our three younger daughters a little later down the road. While we'd say we pretty much raised them the same way as we'd raised our first three kids, we've got to admit what happened. Things did look a little different in the light of a new day.

Mary Beth: For one thing, we were tired.

Steven: Yes, very tired.

Mary Beth: And a little more permissive. But it wasn't so much that we got permissive, I don't think, as much as we just became different in our approach.

Like, one of the funniest things was hearing Emily tell me, "Mom, when I was a kid, *The Bachelorette* was already a thing. It was already in existence. And you no more would've let me watch that show as a teenager than . . ."

And she's right. I wouldn't. And now, here were Stevey Joy and I, bonding over it. "Yeah, exactly!" Emily said. "You sit there and watch it *with* her!"

"Well, you know how it is, Em, I'm just using this opportunity to show her what *not* to do"—which, of course, Emily wasn't buying at all.

But as we thought back on the things we did differently with the later kids, at least in the handful of ways we did it, most of it was like what we've already said. It wasn't really a concerted effort; we were just trying to apply the wisdom of dialing down on some of the *rules,* in favor of focusing in hard on the *relationships.*

Because we had a lot of rules.

And over time, we think we got better—wiser—in terms of how we dealt with TV and movies and stuff. Instead of just being a big *no,* a big censoring service, we told them to think of their viewing and their listening habits like choosing what to eat. When you're determining your diet, the main thing you need for your body is healthy food, things that are good for you. Always focus on that. It doesn't mean you can never have even a single taste of ice cream or candy or some other empty-calorie snack. Just don't ever think you can live on it, that you can survive on junk food alone, because you can't. And yet there are some things available out there, no matter how many other people are consuming them, that are nothing but poison to you. And all of us grow to realize what those things are. So keep away from the poison when you think about what you're ingesting into your life, what you're inviting into your thinking. Because that stuff, no kidding, can kill you.

"Learn to discern." That was another one of those family mottos we used a lot, coming to understand that our main job was training our kids to learn how to tell the good stuff from the bad, more than just telling them what was good and bad—which, we'd like to think, was a little bit of wisdom gained.

It makes you wonder, if you could go back, knowing what you know now, whether your younger self would pass judgment on you, would push back and argue with you, or whether he or she might actually listen to you and maybe discover that not everything they're stressing over is something to go to the mat for. Maybe the younger you would realize the rules are getting in the way of getting to know your kids' hearts, of diving a little deeper into your relationship with them, not just your responsibility for them.

But we get it, how overloaded you feel during that season of life, and how you're just trying to make the complicated less complicated. When our first three were all together, all within four years of each other, we were like, *This is not working! I don't know if we can do this! I don't know if we'll ever experience another peaceful moment as long as we live!* That's how we felt. And the rules made it easier. They gave us less to have to think about somehow.

All of it, all of life, is just enormously complicated, at every step along the way. But what you learn over time is that even though you can't get everything right, and even though you can't make everything easier (in case you were still holding out hope for that), you *can* make it through. There's always hope for *that.*

And you *can* grow wiser.

> *When you say, "God, help me" / you wonder if He's even listening / truth is, I've wondered the very same thing / so you don't have to feel ashamed / let me walk in this valley with you / and tell you all that I've learned to be true*
>
> from "Don't Lose Heart"

One of the things we genuinely considered doing after Maria went to be with Jesus, after the sudden shock of it had worn down to more of a raw simmer, was just to pick up and move somewhere. Maybe even to China. Pull completely out of sight. Be just another foreign person in a world that didn't know us or anything about us. We can't say we thought about it too seriously, not enough to make any real inquiries into how we might possibly pull it off. But it crossed our minds, we can tell you that.

We did, however, do something nearly as drastic.

For the longest time, we couldn't go back home. We stayed with friends. We stayed away. Life had thrown us something so difficult to untangle and realign that we just had no answer for it, no playbook on what to do next.

Emily and her fiancé, Tanner, were set to be married in October, only a few months out. And we were glad they opted not to delay it. We thought it was good and healthy for them, and for all of us, to keep such an important event on the calendar. And by the time we'd added the new memories of a wedding out here on our property, we sort of organically became more and more at peace with the idea of continuing to live here.

Only not. We've written previously about all the hard decisions that went into finally tearing the old house down and building another one—a different one—right here in its old footprint. We still look back and wonder if that was the right thing to do.

It was an answer. It was the answer we decided on and implemented. It was the kind of decision you can't go back on, once you've started it. You have to live with the fallout from it. In this case, the literal fallout.

So, okay, life involves seeking answers for complicated problems. It then involves making decisions based on the answers you conclude are the right ones for those problems. All of us have to deal with this. But in doing it, something comes along that takes the pressure off the huge, human responsibility we all feel for doing things right the first time—something much bigger than right answers and right decisions.

It's something called *sovereignty.*

Sovereignty is the biblical truth that says, "The Lord does whatever he pleases in heaven and on earth" (Ps. 135:6). He is King of all. He is Ruler over everything. He is the one who "gives everyone life and breath," the one who determines our "appointed times" and the circumstances that are taking place around us. "In him we live and move and have our being" (Acts 17:25–28). He knows exactly what we're going through and exactly what He's going to do about it.

Now we're about to get way over our heads theologically, but we're only going to do it for a second, so don't worry. We'll soon return you to our usual rambling.

But *sovereignty.* This is big. The decisions that all of us make when handling complicated situations are real decisions. We are not puppets in a cosmic theater, reading off a script that's already been written for us. Except that, in another sense, every one of our lives is *completely* under our Father's control. "All my days were written in your book and planned before a single one of them began" (Ps. 139:16). "For we are his workmanship, created in Christ Jesus for good works, which God prepared ahead of time for us to do" (Eph. 2:10).

Deep breath here. We can't tell you exactly why or how God does this the way He does it. And anybody who says they *can* tell you the why and the how is overexaggerating their own mental capacity. The sovereignty of God is bigger than our minds can conceive—which is good, because we need Him to be beyond figure-out-able. We'd have a much bigger problem on our hands if He were less smart than us. But as it stands, our job is to be *stewards* of the decisions we make, while we trust Him to be *sovereign* over them—so that, even if we make a *wrong* decision, it's covered under His ability to know exactly how to walk us through it, since He knew it was coming anyway.

God is God and I am not / I can only
see a part of the picture He's painting /
God is God and I am man / so I'll never
understand it all / for only God is God
from "God Is God"

So back to us now and our problem with our big, dumb, complicated calendar.

We don't know what to do. There's no answer to it all. There's appreciation maybe for the other person's point of view. There's understanding of how they could feel the way they feel and why they're so convinced their way of seeing things would make it all so much better if we could just hold our tongues and really listen to them. Perhaps there's even a root desire for accommodating whatever can be accommodated for the sake of peace, no matter how temporary. But rarely does any big workable, long-lasting plan for improvement ever come out of these conversations of ours. Nothing gets solved that can satisfy both of us. And it's no longer even a surprise when it doesn't. That's how complicated it's become.

But here's what wisdom teaches us: "Seek first the kingdom of God and his righteousness, and all these things will be provided for you. Therefore don't worry about tomorrow, because tomorrow will worry about itself. Each day has enough trouble of its own" (Matt. 6:33–34).

Sounds so simple when you say it like that. Do *this*, get *this.* Seek *Him,* be *provided for*. Go into this complicated problem with the primary objective of pleasing Him, and even if it doesn't feel like you've accomplished something on the other side, you've done something important because you've done it for the right reason, by having faith in Him, by trusting what He's said for you to do. And He will see to it that something good comes from it. You may not like where you come down when you can't agree, but we can all agree the Lord will make "all things work together for the good of those who love God, who are called according to his purpose" (Rom. 8:28).

This may not technically be an answer, but one thing's for sure.

There's wisdom there.

Sometimes it's hard to hold you tight / sometimes we feel so far apart / sometimes we dance as one / and feel the beating of each other's heart / some days the dance is slow and sweet / some days we're bouncing off the walls / but no matter how this world may turn / our love will keep us from falling / and we will dance

from "We Will Dance"

This subject of wisdom and truth is central to what we've learned as a couple. Maybe it's what made us willing to put ourselves out there in print like this again. We want to keep sharing what the Lord has shown us and proven to us, both in our successes and (so much more often) in our failures.

Answers aren't the answer. But the *truth* is. The wisdom of truth is what we're searching for in all these chapters.

So when we get to the next one—the chapter we've called "It's the Same, Only Different"—where we'll talk about the stark and severe differences in the way the two of us think and see things, and how much serious trouble we've had in trying to walk a straight line through it, we'll be reminding both you and ourselves that we're *supposed* to be different. It's part of what makes the wonder of husband-and-wife so wonderful—this idea that two people who might hardly ever agree on anything are somehow able to forge a life together. That's a God thing, not an us thing.

Next chapter: Marriage is an ongoing series of "Wins and Losses," of trade-offs and concessions, of receiving and surrendering. It's being humble enough to accept these differences in each other. Not just to accept them but to see what's strangely beautiful about them, even if we don't always see where the other person is coming from.

But marriage is also a place for us to push back, to defend what we believe in. "It's a Fight," and that's okay. That's chapter 5—how something would probably be wrong, dishonest even, if we never found ourselves getting a little (or a lot!) worked up trying to figure out the complicated questions of life together. All these differences set the table for debate. It may not always be a *happy* debate. We should guard against it becoming an *ugly* debate. But it's not milk and cookies. That's make-believe, not marriage.

Life together is just too real for that. "It's a Long Journey" (chapter 6). Don't expect it to wrap up nice and neat before you go to bed tonight. One of us struggled a lot, early on in our marriage, with that "don't let the sun go down on your anger" verse in the Bible, from Ephesians 4. "The sun is down," she'd say, "and I'm still feelin' a lot of anger goin' on here!"

Some of the battles the two of us regularly fight have developed a long story arc. They seem like they've been war zones forever. Yet there's still a path forward toward a future that resembles hope because there's "Ultimately One Decision," the decision to keep showing up (chapter 7). And this "one decision" is what keeps the clock running on redemption, as long as we mix it in with lots and "Lots of Grace" (chapter 8).

"It's a Wonder" how it works (chapter 9).

But "It's Worth It" just the same (chapter 10).

That's where we intend this book to travel as we go forward. And, see, none of the things we've just written here are *answers*—not in these last few paragraphs, not in all the rest of all these chapters. They're not answers. They're truths. They're nuggets of wisdom. They don't tell us specifically how to solve all the problems we're wrangling over, like when the two of us are trying to hammer home our opinions about our ongoing calendar crisis. There's no plug-and-play proposition coming down from on high to save us. And yet the wisdom God can grow in us from the truths He has given us can help all of us do a better job at figuring out how to do marriage better. How to do everything better.

How. Even if we don't know why.

When King David was faced with complicated matters and situations that he had no answers for, he'd apparently taught himself to do something the rest of us can learn from as well. His advice to us when trying to bring the unmanageable down to size was to say, look, "When my heart is overwhelmed, lead me to the rock that is higher than I" (Ps. 61:2 NKJV). Lead me up above points 1, 2, and 3 on some proverbial sermon outline, or the three rules for better communication. Just let me start where God lives, which is way higher than me. Where wisdom occurs. Where He somehow helps us conquer all this complication, even if we don't know how to do it—maybe not in ways that feel good to us in the moment but in ways that please Him and draw us closer together, even if we're still not entirely on the same page.

Imagine David feeling what all of us feel when life gets complicated, when he was totally at a loss about what to do with the troubles that had descended on his life, plus all the troubles he'd been guilty of tangling up into it by himself because of his own foolish foolishness. You can almost see his hands high up in the air in surrender. He's tried and can't do it. There's no way out of this mess, he says—no solution he can see anywhere, not from where he's standing.

"But I trust in you, Lord" (Ps. 31:14). *I trust in You, Lord.*

And when two people can say that to each other in marriage . . .

There's your answer.

Don't get me wrong / I'm still a mess / I've still got a heart with doubts and fears pounding in my chest / I've wrestled, then I've rested / I've trusted, then I've tested God's patience, like a foolish man / but when I surrender once again / and come like a little child reaching up my hands / He lifts me every time and tells me He loves me / still

from "Still"

Chapter 3

It's the Same, Only Different

We told you we've always been Chapmans, both of us. Not just married name but maiden name. Chapman. C-H-A-P-M-A-N.

But put us together, and you can spell our name with one letter. You can name that tune in one note.

That's what the data showed us years ago when we took one of those early personality tests. We'd never been in a counselor's office up until that time. We'd never filled out a questionnaire on our marriage, except maybe for fun in a magazine, to see where we stacked up on a scale of togetherness. But after we'd gone through this first-ever exercise, where we'd input a bunch of answers about how we as individuals each think and operate, we remember the guy sitting down with us and holding up a piece of paper that visually graphed what our information had revealed.

"Here's the problem," he said, or some other abundantly obvious thing, which soon became equally obvious to us. Because as he turned the picture around to where we could see it, the figure on the page looked just like this: X.

One of our curves went *this* way; one of our curves went *that* way. The couple formerly known as the Chapmans were now just . . .

X

X marks the spot! The spot where the trouble begins.

That's how different we are. That's how different the Lord made us. And so that's okay, you could say. Because in His *sovereign* love and wisdom, that's who He created us to be.

Except that He put us together in the same house, in the same life. The same bedroom, the same bathroom, the same family room, the same *every* room. Two people, at cross purposes, crossing paths at just about every place we turn.

And that's where it's *not* been okay.

Not. Okay.

"Well," you may be asking, "how much difference are we talking about?"

Let us count the ways.

Mary Beth	**Steven**
Structured	Unstructured
Half empty	Half full
Linear	Creative
Spreadsheet	Doodle pad
Discerning	Gullible
Realist	Dreamer
Brake pedal	Gas pedal
List maker	Free spirit
I'm worried	What, me worry?
Let's stay	No, let's go!

Can you see the X from where you're sitting?

Now to be fair, it's a lot more complex than the above list might imply. There are plenty of moments and situations where, just like you, we blur the lines and cross over into each other's column. But in general, these are some of the ways we are wired differently. And this kind of wiring can definitely cause some fuses to get blown in marriage.

It hadn't shown up so much when we were first dating. You're not looking for differences then. Or if you do see them, they somehow appear in that context to be sweet, charming, and adorable. Hard to believe now, but that's the truth in the moment. They're what make this other person so interesting, so fascinating, because of how different they are. Their differences create a flavor for things that you haven't really felt or thought about much before, things you may even secretly wish were different about *you,* if you weren't so "structured/unstructured," if you weren't so "half empty/half full."

But then you get married. And these differences are suddenly not so *engaging* anymore. Now you're living with them. And stuck with them. There's no getting around them.

Stop us if you know what we're talking about because we're pretty sure it's something you struggle with in your marriage too, if you're married. "Opposites attract," as they say, although hopefully the diagram drawn from your test answers would form a much prettier letter than our big fat X. Still, we'd imagine you clash with each other at one or more hard angles on a fairly regular, fairly daily basis. You're different people in those ways. And where that's true, you'd probably say it's become a primary source of conflict in your home, if not just consternation, these differences in your temperaments, in your makeup, in your perspectives.

Like in that list of personal differences we just showed you. Those are ours. To put them into broader categories, think of one of us as the twinkle-eyed, energetic, boundlessly optimistic type who sees hope and opportunity around every corner, then is naturally inclined to go chase nearly every opportunity with a forgetful neglect for the clock or for pretty much any other quantifiable structure of measurement. Think of the other one of us, on the other hand, as the calendar and the spreadsheet, the careful planner, analyzer, and researcher, the nice-and-tidy housekeeper who'd love nothing more than having everything in its place, the flowers and the garden planted, whose main standard of measure is the semifearful, semicynical outlook that sees problems first, sees potential later.

What could possibly go wrong in *this* marriage?

What about yours?

Well, one thing that could happen is: You might develop an infuriating desire for *changing* this other person into someone who looks a little more like you, who thinks a little more like you, who makes plans a little more like you, and who basically does all the things the way you want them done, without needing to be talked into it, coerced into it, or guilted into it.

But that's the differences talking. And they can get so intense and ugly. Again, infuriating. Because differences are determined not to get along. Left to themselves, they *can't* get along. Unless something acts on them, unless we act to counteract them. Unless somebody does something.

Something *different.*

I am Tarzan / you are Jane / I am night and you are the day / like sunshine and rain / we're so different from each other / you are woman / I am man / you're the sea and I am the land / and I would not be who I am / if I didn't have you

from "We Belong Together"

One of the best ways we've found in trying to solve for X in our marriage equation has come from trying to twist it around into another kind of geometric shape. What if we could look at the X and see a triangle?

We were told, like you were probably told, to think of the marriage relationship that way. Like a triangle. First, imagine the husband and wife represented by the two separate points at the bottom, down there at the two hinges on the lower part, down at the base of it. From this vantage point, we can see we're living inside the same space, the same shape, we're sharing a cohesive relationship, and yet we're still capable of being a good distance away from each other in a lot of different aspects. Imagine God, then, represented by the other point of the triangle, the highest point, the one that's located above and immovably between the two.

In this model, if we're both trying to get closer to Him—if we're each climbing the arms on either side of that triangle, moving continually in His direction as followers of Jesus—then when we stand back and look at it, we'll see we've not only drawn closer to *Him* (vertically), we've drawn closer to each other too (horizontally). We're not quite as far apart as when we were both down at the bottom, when we were both existing in our own different places and headspaces, separated by that long line of differences between us.

We think this is a great analogy. It's what we strive for; and, ultimately, it's what we most desire—moving closer to God and letting Him and His Word shape us and bring us closer to each other.

In our marriage, though, we've added to this first triangle a second triangle. (It's the one we move toward on those days when, honestly, one or the other of us is maybe *not* getting closer to God.) On this triangle, the center point is just survival. We've got to get through the day. We've got to figure out whatever problem or circumstance is bearing down on us at the moment. We're tired of fighting, tired of butting heads, tired of feeling the blood pressure rising on another day of feeling diametrically opposed to each other. I want to do it *this* way; you want to do it *that* way. But *either* way, we've got to get this figured out and figured out soon. Preferably MY WAY. But how?

So put yourself inside this little scenario for a second. Let's say you're a ten-minutes-early-is-on-time kind of person, and your spouse is about to make you late getting somewhere again. Tell us which outcome is worse: (1) showing up to wherever you're going a couple of minutes later than you were expected, or (2) making the whole car ride over there a lecture to a grown human being about planning ahead better and using his or her time more appropriately. (Along with probably some other talking points. Less helpful ones.)

Now if you're new to marriage, or even if you're a somewhat veteran couple by now—five, ten, fifteen years—we're not sure it's fair to expect of you what we're about to share. But as two people who've been doing this for forty years, having been through a bazillion of these types of situations, the time finally arrives when the effort it costs to contest these differences in mindset, or sensitivity, or internal clock, or whatever, becomes just more trouble than it's worth. And in an amazing turnaround—yes, you'll be *amazed* seeing yourself do this!—you not only give your spouse a little more permission to be themselves, but you oddly become a little more identical to them your *own* self.

Like, if you're the one who runs ten or fifteen minutes behind as a rule, you start to notice you're beginning to adjust your old habits and are becoming a little more punctual. Like *them.* And if you're the one who'd rather pour salt in an open wound than not be in your seat when an event starts, not having to climb over people who are already there, the people who got there on time, like people are supposed to do . . .

You see what we mean.

You don't do it because you *want* to, and you don't do it to be nice. You do it because you *have* to—because turning yourself into a fashionably late person may be what it takes to be a "still here" kind of person.

Partly, it comes from discovering that your wife or husband's inborn defaults are maybe not so wacko to begin with. They seem to work for *them* anyway; maybe you could learn to make them work for you too. But partly, like we said, you've just gotta survive. If you can't beat 'em, join 'em.

Granted, this triangle is drawn in the shape of surrender. It's not even really that crisp of a design. It's not sharply creased at the corners. The times when we've drawn it, you can tell we were feeling some serious life fatigue. But in this version of the triangle, in this effort to survive, the two of us have noticed many of our X-shaped differences have slowly started straightening out. A little bit. We do hope we're still becoming more like Jesus, like in the first triangle, as we inch our way up the ladder, as we let His grace make us a little more godly. We really do. But we are also becoming, in a surprising twist, a little more like each other too. A little less *different.*

That's the magic of the second triangle.

It's how the one of us who at first didn't understand the concept of washing a bath towel—figuring you're never cleaner than when you're getting out of the shower, so what does the towel need washing for?—is now the person who makes our bed every morning, the way the *other* one of us used to do it. And the one whose laptop home screen looks as if the digital cleaning crew just got finished waving their magic wand of organization over it, leaving every file folder meticulously labeled and coded and stacked just so, has discovered you can still be next to godliness even if you can't see the floor of your closet.

The one of us who was the *least* organized now gets an E for some amazing effort at becoming at least organized-*ish,* after a fashion. And the one who was the most "stick-in-the-mud" about staying on a schedule and streamlining every process has developed the ability, albeit with her eye twitching a bit, not to notice the mess.

There's been some real shape-shifting going on here.

Now some would describe this minitransformation by using a word like *settling.* "You're settling." Okay, some of it *is* just settling. Some of what used to drive that "infuriating desire" of yours, where you sought to will the other person into seeing and responding to life the way *you* see and respond to it, has sort of hollowed out for you into more of a silent heartache. Because after forty years, you know it's not going to happen. And it can make you feel sad. It can leave you feeling distant and disappointed in your marriage, convinced that even with both of you saying you're committed to becoming more accommodating toward each other, you are still the one who's making the *most* changes, and that your spouse—especially in those places where you're seeing *no* change—has just given up trying. Now maybe they *have*; maybe they *haven't.* If you could know what they really think, maybe you'd realize they've not given up at all, that they're as burdened by your distance and disappointment as *you* are. Maybe you'd realize they are doing their best to blend your differences together without having to turn their mind completely off and simply take orders from you, like you're some sort of tyrant or something.

Okay, this is starting to sound like one of our counseling sessions, talking about the big topic that has dominated so many of those clinical discussions. All we know for sure is that we tried for the longest time doing things the way we naturally preferred to do them, or else. We were always ready to fight each other for it. But that's just it: We found these stylistic differences had turned into constant battlegrounds. Into nonstop war in the homeland. Into nothing but trouble in the heartland. It's true we've not been willing to come to terms on *all* the differences that have gotten us crossways with each other over the years. But in some of the ones that we could realistically concede without giving up a piece of ourselves that seemed too essential to part with, we've found a path for meeting in the middle. Imperfectly but, more and more often, peaceably.

The *triangle* has had a wonderful way of slowly rounding off some of the sharp edges on us both and helping us come to see that we actually fit together in some pretty remarkable ways.

For us, this decision boils down to a truth, to a bit of biblical wisdom, that we feel sure we'll mention again and again in later chapters because it's become such a consistent theme that we've tried to model in our marriage. We've *tried.* Give us that.

Paul, in Ephesians 4, was turning the page from the Paul who'd been writing Ephesians 1–3. That's the part where he'd been telling the early believers everything God had done to turn us from miserable sinners, doomed to destruction, into redeemed sinners saved by His kindness and love. "For you are saved by grace through faith, and this is not from yourselves; it is God's gift" (Eph. 2:8). It is all *Him*, not *us.* The reason we can live like completely new people on the other side of being saved is because we are now superpowered by "him who is able to do above and beyond all that we ask or think" (Eph. 3:20). That's some really good news.

Then comes chapter 4, where Paul started to tell us *exactly* how our lives can be different now that God's Spirit is living inside us. By His power, we can function with qualities like "humility and gentleness." Wouldn't those look good on a marriage? And "with patience." That's another key principle, another fruit of the Spirit. Patience makes one of the best-tasting differences ever in the lives of two drastically different people who find themselves sharing the same last name.

(Of course, because we're "us," there's even been debate at times—good-natured, mind you—about whose name we're actually sharing, since we've both been Chapmans all our lives. "Am I sharing my name with *you*? Are you sharing your name with *me*?")

But our favorite line from Ephesians 4 is the last little phrase of that second verse, where Paul says in addition to developing such life-changing traits as humility, gentleness, and patience, we can also download the power of something else, the experience of . . .

"bearing with one another in love."

There you go. "Bear with one another in love." Remember that phrase. It may just be the whole secret to what makes marriages work.

"Bearing with one another in love" is why that second triangle is not just a cop-out, why it's not an acting job where you're pretending to be accommodating to your spouse while letting the same level of contempt keep simmering underneath. It's not about changing yourself for effect. Or at least we hope not. It's about deciding to choose love over personal preferences.

To bear the agitation.

To do something *different* about these differences.

And to do it in love.

This is what *God* loves, helping us be patient and kind, not rude and irritable, not keeping a record of wrongs, but *bearing* all things—that's how 1 Corinthians 13 says it, the love chapter—until "bearing with one another" becomes a loving habit.

Now He obviously wouldn't tell us to make these higher choices if there wasn't something hard and heavy to be borne, if the frustrations that have accumulated in our relationship didn't truly exist, as if we were making them all up. No, they're real. And they're rough.

In fact, they're even worse than we know. One of the unexpected observations you glean after being together a long time is that this person you married is different not only in the ways you've always known them to be, not only in the "structured/unstructured" categories that have helped you put their tendencies into identifiable buckets. The truth is, you're both changing all the time. He or she really *isn't* the same person you married, not after what life has done to them over the years.

We've read a lot of books on marriage, but this specific insight is one we've only begun seeing and figuring out for ourselves as we go. People will say, as part of their rationale for pulling away from their marriage, "He's just not the same person I married anymore," or "She's turned into someone I would never have married if I'd known she was going to change like this." There's a lot of deception going on when someone says those things, when they start believing the lie that says they've outgrown their mate. But there's also a whole lot of truth in what they say, in this novel idea that he or she—as well as each one of us—is not exactly the same man or woman as before.

Life changes you.

Dramatically.

It changes *him*.

It changes *her*.

Becoming a mom, for example, changes you. This woman who used to focus her affection almost exclusively on her husband is now pouring it into another person, often soon into multiple little persons. And it changes the DNA of her heart for the rest of her life. She's a mom now. She's different.

You see something similar happening in a man, when a husband becomes a dad. He takes on a new role and responsibility that, in most cases, he didn't possess when the two of you met.

But while parenting is the biggest way, or at least the most common way people change in marriage across the board, it's hardly the only life event that carries this level of impact. *Stress* changes you. *Grief* changes you. The traumas you go through and encounter in life, whether all at once or as an ongoing accumulation of unwanted and unwelcome things—they change you. They recolor you. They rewire your brain. They shake things up inside of you that often require a next-level degree of God's wisdom and grace to understand.

It's just never as simple as being, you know, introvert versus extrovert. Type A and type B. Each of those personality differences contains its own challenges, flare-ups, and work-arounds, for sure. But they become almost cake when compared with the newcomers that gradually worm their way in—the anxiety, the panic, the insomnia, the physical limitations—the ones you didn't even know to be looking for. Like, where did *that* come from?

But here's the thing: If you'll hang on through the changes—through the years when it's the hardest to find the humility, gentleness, and patience to bear these new arrivals in love—you might discover, on the other side, not only the person you first fell in love with, but even more of what makes this person you fell in love with so extraordinary. Despite all the differences, and despite all the changes, you might experience God giving you back the person you've been patiently (or, at times, not so patiently) bearing with.

We're not sure we've communicated even yet to you just how much crap and grief we've waded through together in our years of marriage. Whatever aura of brightness and prettiness you may have painted around your picture of us, you might not believe how wrong you are. And much of the trouble we've had—nearly all of it, really—has found its source in these loud, blaring Xs of differences between us. Our holy wedlock has too often become something more like "holy headlock!"

We've been a mess at times . . . a BIG mess.

Now none of the various counselors we've sat under have ever advised us to end our marriage over it, using those exact words. No one's ever come right out and said that. But we are pretty sure if we'd ever gone that far, if we'd ever made that choice, some of those counselors would've encouraged us we were making the best decision. The vibe we received from them at times, from certain ones of them, is that there truly are marriages where the severity of the struggle and the difficulty and the differences is more than a couple can carry, and that maybe ours was one of them.

We only mention this embarrassing truth to you in case our attempt at describing the X on our survey page sounded almost cute when you heard it, like "bless their hearts." No. It has not blessed our hearts. It's just about torn our hearts into pieces too many times.

But we also mention it for another reason. A better reason. Again, don't hear us saying we're not still wrestling with our differences. We are. We do. This year, in some ways, has been like every other year, like every battle gone before. Still the same.

And yet, the good thing about its still being the same is that at least it means we're still here. And maybe on some days, it means our little triangle thingy is doing its job.

We recently took off on a fun, spontaneous outing that—not both of us, but one of us—had always wanted to undertake: the great 400 Mile Sale. *Yard* sale. It snakes along Highway 68, across the entire state of Kentucky, eventually taking in about twenty counties on its way from the Ohio state line (Mary Beth's home state), down through Paducah (Steven's hometown), and on to where western Kentucky empties out into eastern Missouri.

And it was . . . you know, it was one yard sale after another, like you'd expect. Which is awesome and kind of cool for a while. Until you've done enough of them.

But we did them together. For a few stop-and-go days, which we shortened by a day from the original plan, we hung in there and followed the tacky handwritten signs from one junk sale to the next. (Notice the give-and-take, see, by the planner person, who let us stop at only *three* days. Thank you!) We looked through stuff that people had decided they didn't want, and we bought a few samples of it that we decidedly didn't need. It wasn't what you'd call a great success, as far as finding any valuable treasures. But we had a big time. We laughed ourselves silly through most of it.

We acted goofy, like we used to do. We talked and entertained ourselves in between. We tried to listen to a marriage book in the car on audio, thinking it sounded like a productive thing to do while we drove. Wouldn't that have made us look noble on Instagram? But we eventually gave up even on that, when one of us found it a little too boring. (Give-and-take, again, by the person who came up with the audiobook idea, not insisting we finish it.)

The triangle helps. The triangle works.

But you've got to live it out. You've got to stay here long enough to see it take shape. It doesn't happen overnight. You've got to keep pressing in and pressing on. You've got to get the "bear" out of your system on the way to "bearing" it all in love. And you've got to commit to staying inside of it, inside this four-hundred-mile marathon that will eventually, if you keep doing it, take you to some amazing places you've always wanted to go.

So please, please tell me what you can /
'cause I want to understand / how does
it look from your side / how does it look
from where you are / how does it look from
your side / from your side of the world
from "Your Side of the World"

Mary Beth: I've said it many times, and it's still true: There's a real part of me that would've preferred marrying an accountant, not a creative. I didn't realize fully at first, just starting out, what it was going to be like, not being able to count on the predictable rhythm of dad coming in the door at 4:30 every afternoon, sitting down to dinner, mowing the grass on the weekend, changing the oil every three months or three thousand miles. That's the way I grew up.

And, sure, I didn't expect or even want Steven's and my marriage to identically mirror that. I enjoyed the variety and excitement of what he and his music career brought to my life. But as time went on, and as the wheel of unknowns really got spinning, the part of me that likes things scheduled and patterned began to feel threatened, like I was losing control. And out of my frustration, I was constantly fighting not to be robbed of something valuable that was important to me. Both important and good. Important and, to my mind, necessary.

Steven: That's part of what I've always questioned about myself and our marriage. I know the Lord brought Mary Beth and me together by His design—we're completely convinced of that. We make our plans but God directs our steps, right? Like it says in Proverbs? But, honestly, I've thought at times, *God, really?* She needed someone so much better than me, in terms of being better organized, in terms of thinking differently, in terms of processing life a certain way. I'm just not the right person for her. "What in the world, God, were You thinking?"

Mary Beth: I appreciate Steven's sensitivity to that. I've also come to appreciate (on some days) the things he does and the way he thinks that are different to how I do them and how I think. I sort of envy, for example, his ability to approach life in his "bouncy, bouncy" Tigger-like way, to not be so convinced that things are as "oh, bother" Eeyore-ish as they sometimes appear to be. To me. These parts of his nature have sort of worn off on me, I think, the same way my realistic "we need a plan" mentality has sort of gotten into his bloodstream a little as well. Hasn't it? Tell me it has.

The part, I guess, where I still struggle with him the most now—and, I'll admit, it's probably the sin in me—is just feeling this need for appreciation coming back to me that says, "Hey, I see how hard you're working on this; I recognize what it's costing you to 'bear with me' in these areas."

Because, honestly, I feel less resistance now in terms of assimilating some of my wants and expectations to his. I don't think I'm nearly as adamant as I used to be about getting my way or making a huge angry deal about it. I just want him to notice I'm doing it. It would mean a lot to hear him say to me, more often than he says it, "I know this isn't how you want it. I know you'd like the house just right and the schedule just right. You've laid down so much, waiting for our life to look the way you'd like it to look." Because I have. It does feel like I've "settled" sometimes from pursuing my ideals, which is a bad feeling for someone like me. So, can this just be said? "Thank you"? That'd mean a lot to me.

Steven: That's fair. And good. And true. I certainly don't want to ever have the attitude of, "You know, sweetheart, this is just how it is. This is who I am," and expect her to be fine with it. I also know neither of us wants to be the one who says or ever implies to the other, "This thing of yours"—her hunger for structure, predictability, and control; my heart for creativity and spontaneity—"it has to die if you expect to keep me happy."

Let's just say it this way: "You need to change" (*you*, meaning your wife or husband) is not a successful strategy for people who want their marriage to have staying power. That's not to say each of us shouldn't be serious about scaling that triangle, being willing to grow, adapt, and change *ourselves* as much as possible, all in a humble and God-honoring desire to show our spouse how much we value them. To bear with them in love.

But let's be honest. We are different. It's part of what makes marriage hard; it's also part of what makes marriage happen. As someone has famously said, in a quote that's been attributed wildly to everyone from Henry Ford to Winston Churchill: "If two people agree on everything, one of them is unnecessary." If marriage is meant to be a living picture of the gospel (and it is!), much of its purpose and beauty comes from showing the world how people who may naturally have few things in common can still be united by something (by Someone) they *both* share in common.

It takes these differences of ours to make marriage add up to something that's better than both of us.

I know that somedays / we both wonder how we ever got together / we're still so different now / but I can't imagine my life without you / 'cause all those things that make us so different / are just what make us all that we are

from "We Belong Together"

Chapter 4

It's Wins and Losses

Have you ever felt like you got married on the wrong end of your life? Like, if you could somehow start over again with at least some of the perspective you've gained over the years, you're sure you could make (and would've made) so many things go so much better.

But what are you saying, when you say that? You're saying your life—the one you're living right now—is not what it should've been. It's not what it could've been. It's lacking. It's less than. It's messed up. It's not right.

And you know what? You *are* right. Or at least you're somewhat right. Some of the things that have happened, some of the ways it's worked out, some of the decisions you've made, some of the goals you thought were worth whatever it cost to achieve them—not all of them have ended up being assets on your balance sheet of life. Some of them, maybe even a whole big pile of them, have globbed up in what you now consider your liability column. And you'd give anything if you could go back and exchange them for something better.

So, okay, your marriage, like our marriage—your life, like our life—has not been a long, unbroken winning streak. It hasn't been one undefeated season after another, after another. But that's not to say it can't still be or can't still become a good story, with a good ending, even without the available option of going back to the beginning and starting all over again.

It's just that winning may look quite a bit different today than we envisioned when we were first starting out, way back when. Your and our definition of it—what winning is supposed to look like in our home, how it's supposed to feel, where it's supposed to take us, and who we're supposed to be when we get there—may not match up with what the voices in our ear told us to expect winning to be when we were twenty-five.

Because here's what we've found. Most of the winning that happens in our marriage happens when we start accepting some losses. It comes to us in those hard-fought areas where we've learned (or are trying to learn) to give in, where we've chosen (or are trying to choose) to give up—the places where, without our realizing it, we've actually been chasing victory away by fighting so hard to win what we each thought we wanted.

Giving up what I can't keep anyway / to gain something that I know I'll never lose / trading in the temporary for the eternal / and though it's settled, I'm reminded every day / to live or die to self, it's up to me to choose / so if I

want to win the fight, there's a part of me
that must die / well, I've said my goodbyes
from "Dying to Live"

Now really this topic is much bigger than just marriage. It's a whole-life principle.

Losing to win.

We all like to run toward those Bible verses that talk about, you know, abundant life and overcoming, about being restored from the locust-eaten folly of our ways. And all of that is true, thank God, because of how He chooses to honor the greatness of His grace and how in His mercy He gives good things to His people. He made us for joy. He made us to enjoy Him. As we learned from our pastor Scotty Smith years ago, quoting from the Westminster Shorter Catechism, "Man's chief end is to glorify God and enjoy Him forever."

But you cannot focus in on the joyous, victorious heritage of the saints without viewing it through the prism of what Jesus called true discipleship. "If anyone wants to follow after me, let him deny himself," He said, "for whoever wants to save his life will lose it, but whoever loses his life because of me will find it" (Matt. 16:24–25). The apostle Paul, same thing. He talked about how the "surpassing value of knowing Christ Jesus my Lord" was worth suffering "the loss of all things," giving up *anything* if it would help him "gain Christ" (Phil. 3:8–9).

We win by losing.

It's how we find what really matters.

But while this backwards path to winning is not *confined* to marriage, it does have a bearing on what *defines* our marriage.

We're of the mind that marriage can still have its magic moments. We can hope, can't we? Just because people grow up and grow old doesn't mean there's no more Cinderella and Prince Charming. We can still aspire to love and to dance and to watch our dreams come true. We are children of our heavenly Father, and fathers love blessing their kids with the pure and beautiful desires of their hearts.

But marriage, at the true depths of its soul, cannot be built around these things: living our dreams, getting what we want, expecting to always go from one achievement and ambition to the next. It's certainly not what any of us can expect to experience individually: having no one to say no to us, no one to have a different opinion from ours, no one to hold the line on reality, no one to slow down our pursuit of things that aren't good or valuable for us, or for both of us as a couple.

God's main business with you, like His main business with us, is to keep shaping us in holiness. To keep making us more like Jesus, whatever it takes. Which, as it turns out, may not be the road we thought we were setting out on, but it's the road that leads us to the fullest and most satisfying life of all.

The Bible's word for it is to *sanctify* us. "This is God's will, your sanctification" (1 Thess. 4:3). Because, let's be honest, we are not the people we want to be yet. We know it. Surely God knows it. And like any father—especially the greatest Father—He wants to see us become all we were created to be. He'll do anything to grow us in holiness. To sanctify us.

He can do this, of course, through all kinds of ways, most of them ways we'd never choose for ourselves if we were the ones choosing. Because they're usually costly and uncomfortable. And largely counterintuitive. You've been in some of those places before, like we have. They're not a lot of fun, are they. They don't appear, on their face, to be pathways to goodness and blessing. The hard places. The tight places. The pride-busting, self-effacing places.

How interesting, though—how cosmically ingenious—the fact that God's chosen method for leading us out onto the toughest sanctification practice field of all is marriage. He lets us choose it *ourselves*! He makes us unwittingly want it, falling crazy in love enough with another person until all we can think about is marrying them and spending the whole rest of our lives together with them. We willingly walk the aisle, choosing to share our innermost being with this man or this woman for a lifetime, not realizing the package deal we've just accepted.

Now He's got us where He wants us.

Scripture talks so often about how God's sanctifying work in our lives is a "refining" process—a refining fire, refining the hard edges off us. A major objective for why He puts us together in marriage is to pare down those parts of us that need smoothing out or even to burn down the ones that need a complete changing out. It's all part of making us more like Christ, getting the blockages out of the way that are preventing Him from living His life through us.

"Many will be purified, cleansed, and refined," the Bible says, and "those who have insight will understand" (Dan. 12:10). If we look at it the way God looks at it, we'll know He's doing it for our good. He's doing it to make us better.

He's doing it to help us win.

And I will be here / when the laughter turns to crying / through the winning, losing, and trying / we'll be together / 'cause I will be here

from "I Will Be Here"

So losing. Now we're back to this idea we talked about in the last chapter. Giving in. Giving up. Settling. Is that the only reason the two of us have been able to stay together this long? Is it because we just finally, at some point, got too tired to fight back?

Yes.

(Okay, not yes.) Sometimes yes.

But, no, it's just that as you get older, as you get farther away from the starting line, you realize there's no magic wand you can wave over your wife or husband to get them to do what you want. Nor is there any airtight program of reform you can impose on yourselves as a couple (or on yourself as an individual) that suddenly eliminates all the ingredients that have made your marriage such a struggle all this time. You've already tried all that. You've tried everything. Still, here you are.

You're here now where this situation—this not-how-I-wanted-everything-to-be situation—could go one of two ways. It could get all balled up with bitterness and blaming and cynicism and regret, where you're constantly frustrated with yourself, your spouse, and your children, knowing that a number of different choices, on your part or someone else's part—or maybe everybody else's part—could've kept you from getting here. (We're getting out of breath just thinking about it.)

Or . . .

You can give.

Give in. Give up.

But giving doesn't feel good. It may even create the feeling that you're a fake, that you're playing a mind game with yourself that you know you can't follow through on. If you make any move toward chilling out—especially in a contested subject area where you've been notorious for digging in your heels before—you may think it's going to turn you into a person you don't even recognize anymore.

It's just one big loss. One big lose.

Losing ground. Losing leverage. Losing face. Losing control. Losing advantage.

Except that the alternative, when you think about it, is a whole lot worse. Losing sleep. Losing energy. Losing your temper. Losing your patience. Losing heart. Losing hope. Losing love. And maybe losing each other too—maybe not in an official way but just in a creeping ooze of distance and dislike, of discord and disapproval, all of it roaming around on eggshells through the house.

There's just so much to lose.

By not losing.

Losing what? Well, like, losing the "my way is the right way" mentality, the "here's how it's got to be" kind of attitude—losing the sense of pride and superiority that keeps us from leaning into a posture of humility and teachability.

Or losing the complaining. The judgment statements. The assumptions of what the other one is thinking. The damaging references to the past that are so tempting to bring back up. Can't we just lose those? Give the benefit of the doubt once in a while? Be forgiving? Pursue peace where it's possible? Cross off some of the expectations we carry around? Are all of them really worth the fight? Because maybe they're not as essential to our well-being as we've always built them up to be.

We do want to be careful, though, in talking about *losing,* not to pretend we know the exact context you're living in as you're reading this. We're talking here about incorporating a reflex of restraint into our default settings. Learning the value of a thoughtful pause. That's generally a good thing. We're talking about developing a bias toward checking our own desires and agendas before we've turned them into explicit demands. That's a good thing too.

But we are *not* talking about succumbing to abusive treatment from a dominant spouse. We are *not* talking about allowing yourself to cower beneath your human worth because of a toxic imbalance of power in your home.

In fact, in case it was starting to sound like we were writing a little too flippantly and high-mindedly about all this, here are a few winning "losses" we've found to be equally vital in keeping us together.

Sometimes, we've learned, for our marriage to get better and healthier, we need to lose some of the lies we've been believing about ourselves. Let's talk for a second about a common position a lot of us assume when life at home is mostly hard days and lots of conflict and other things we can't seem to get past.

We think it's all our fault.

First, a biblical disclaimer: "There is no one righteous, not even one" (Rom. 3:10). We are all bad people. We are all infected by sin, way down deep inside of us. We are all to blame to some degree for some of the disharmony and dysfunction that exists in our relationships. Even if the other person has done something really bad, we may not be responsible for why they did *that,* but we are still responsible for what we *have* done that hasn't been so great either.

And yet . . .

It's not all our fault. We are not the whole problem. The burden for fixing whatever's broken in our marriage or in our family is not 100 percent on *us*, no matter what any other person may say.

And maybe it's time we lost that. The "I guess it's all me" state of the union. Because it doesn't come from as holy and humble a place as we sometimes think it does. It's not as blatantly true as it often seems, at those times when we're the most depressed or when we're trying to be the most honest and undiluted and unbiased with ourselves.

Certainly we would all do well to change some things. But even if we could change *all* the things about ourselves that are not what they should be or are not what they should've been, it still wouldn't be enough. We wouldn't suddenly discover that everything and everyone is at total peace all around us, now that we've fixed the part that was all wrong about it. (Us.) We are *part* of what's wrong here. We are *part* of the conflict. But we are not the sum of all failures. We are not the sole obstacle between our current living situation and a more satisfying family life and marriage.

"You are not enough" is not what wisdom says to you.

It's what your *enemy* says to you. "You don't have what it takes. You'll *never* have what it takes. You are the worst excuse for a wife/husband, a mother/father there's probably ever been. Look at you. What you've done. You don't think you should be so hard on yourself? You're not being hard *enough* on yourself! If you were harder on yourself, maybe you'd finally get a clue about the real reason things have been falling apart around here the way they've been."

Know the feeling? Recognize that voice?

Now maybe that's not, for you, how the trains of thought usually travel through your head. Maybe the more common arguments you hear in your mind are the ones that challenge you to defend yourself and make excuses for yourself, to fill your quiver with juicy arrows that'll sting when you interject them into your next pointed conversation.

But if self-condemnation is something you find yourself tempted to run toward, as we do, be careful it doesn't push you past the limits of true repentance. Because as surely as we all could stand to lose the hard edge that we use when evaluating each other's imperfections—Lord, help us, yes—we could all benefit from losing the expectation that the answer to all our problems is found in achieving our own perfection. Being better is always a win, but demanding ourselves to be *perfect* is always a loss.

Marriage is not one person changing for the other.

Marriage is two people bearing with each other in love.

That's been a win in our book.

And while we're on a roll here, let's talk about another "loss" that's become rather critical for us and is probably critical for everyone. It was important enough to Jesus that He brought it up on at least one occasion during His teaching ministry. And it had already been important enough for God not to wait any later than the second or third page of the Bible to introduce it.

Leaving and *cleaving*.

Adam and Eve had only just met, two verses earlier, before God said their marriage represented why "a man leaves his father and mother and bonds with his wife, and they become one flesh" (Gen. 2:24)—which is interesting because, unlike us, they didn't even *have* a father or mother. Sounds like He was directing this statement more to *us* than to *them*.

But to many people, this transfer of priority from parents to spouse is a huge undertaking, a major change of mindset. Practically impossible in places, with a cost that seems too high for some.

Maybe you could tell us of times when the tug-of-war between these lifelong attachments to parents has led to some harmful and hurtful strains in your attachment to each other in marriage. We can think of several key moments in our own life together when we've been faced with making a definitive choice to put each other—my wife, my husband—ahead of what either one of our families of origin might have been wanting of us or suggesting to us in the moment.

Steven: I remember, for example, early in our marriage, a conversation I had one day with my dad. We'd gone out fishing, which is one of our favorite things to do together. But I'd told Mary Beth, before Dad and I left that morning, that I'd be home by a certain time. And as the day began to wear on, I started dropping subtle hints every so often about how I'd be needing to head back pretty soon.

My dad, great as he is, has never been one to carefully monitor the time, especially

> when fishing is involved, so I knew he wouldn't naturally pick up on the sense of urgency or importance I was trying to convey. He was half kidding, I'm sure, but was probably half prodding a little as well, when he said, after spinning another long cast far out into the water, "Who wears the pants in that family of yours?"
>
> Typical, right? The typical response of a man from my dad's generation. But I remember, hearing him say it, feeling like there was more to it than just that. I seemed to know, in the moment, that this conversation we were having was going to redefine what my relationship with him was going to be like in the future.
>
> It was hard for me to do. Standing up to my dad wasn't (and still isn't) in my normal makeup, and pleasing him has always been high on my list of priorities. But on that day, I decided to push back. I remember respectfully telling him, "Well, Dad, I put on my pants and try to honor what I've told my wife so she knows she can count on me. It's important to her. And she's important to me. So that's what 'wearing the pants' looks like in our family."

It's simply true that marriages can never be as united as they need to be if anyone else is as important to us as we are to each other. Anyone else's opinions. Anyone else's expectations. They're not *un*important, but they cannot be equally or more important than those of your wife or husband.

And this goes for other family and friends too. Remember the old TV show *This Is Us*? The finale episode ended with the two brothers and the sister sharing a sweet and beautiful moment, telling each other (something like), "When I think about family, the first thing I think about is you guys." Well, good, for television. Sounds so special. But in real life, the first thing either one of us should think about, when we think about family, is us. "This is us."

You come first, sweetheart, you come first. And there's no higher place for anyone else to rank than a nice but close second. Not your children, not your parents, your favorite sibling, or your favorite friend. (Sorry.) Love and care for them to the end, but always remember who comes first. For the win.

In the book *Life Worth Living*, written by a trio of Yale University professors, and based on the enormously popular class they continue to offer and teach to their Ivy League students, the authors let us sit in on their collegiate-level course as readers.[1] What indeed is a "Life Worth Living"? they ask, exploring the answer through the lives and words of people throughout history.

Among their observations is that our Western view of "the good life" is encapsulated in the commercial slogan once popularized by the drugstore chain Walgreens: "At the Corner of Happy and Healthy." This cheery little sound bite, intended to influence people's choice of pharmacies, does kind of capture what the typical red-blooded American considers success: a long, happy, and healthy life.

But are those the right and best terms to use? Is this really what we're all supposed to be shooting for? If we could just be happy. If we could just be healthy. For a long, long time.

We'd have it all.

We think.

But if you look back, as their book does, through the lives of people who've made some of the most enormous contributions to the world, whose lives continue to inspire generations long after their deaths, you discover in so many cases the raw suffering they went through, the losses they endured, their painful struggles against sometimes crippling health conditions, and for some of them, an early death. Jesus Himself, though contented and happy in relationship with His Father, was a man of sorrows, acquainted with grief, ill-treated by both friends and enemies, and murdered at thirty-three. Yet can anyone say He didn't succeed at living?

Maybe the corner of happy and healthy isn't necessarily the ultimate goal we've been encouraged to believe it is.

We can think we know the level of health and happiness that's required as a precondition to our winning. We can insist that marriage be all romance and red roses, fun and laughter, healthy children and a comfortable someone to spend our old age with. And God in His love and mercy may give us some of those things, even all of those things. But, thankfully, He's got much bigger and infinitely better plans for us than that.

Holiness, not just *happiness*.

One of our favorite teachers and mentors, Tim Keller, who is now with Jesus, left us a quote that we've hung on the living room wall of our hearts: "If we want to be happy in marriage, we will accept that marriage is designed to make us holy, not happy. Happiness is a byproduct."[2]

Boom . . . mic drop!

This is the good life. And according to the Bible, this is love.

"Love is patient, love is kind" (1 Cor. 13:4). But how do we ever learn to get those words out of the Bible and into our marriage, unless we're given opportunities to practice both patience and kindness—to *lose* something?

Love is "not rude, is not self-seeking, is not irritable, and does not keep a record of wrongs" (v. 5). But how do we know true love without being put into situations where it takes everything within us—what only Jesus can put there by His grace—not to be rude and self-centered, to be the scorekeeper of all wrongdoings?

Love "bears all things" (v. 7). It makes us willing, by remembering what His love bore for us, to say, in those moments when we're really not in a giving mood with each other, "Thank You, Jesus, for this opportunity to identify more with You and with what it means to lay down my life for You." There's a win there, if you want it, because "blessed is the one who isn't offended by me," Jesus said (Matt. 11:6)—the ones who've come to realize there's a lot more to be gained by giving up than by giving grief.

C. S. Lewis (another one of our favorites) said it best, as usual: "Put first things first and we get second things thrown in: put second things first and we lose both first and second things."[3] Joy in marriage comes from giving when we'd rather get, from backing off when we'd rather barge in, from surrendering our rights to "second things" that we've elevated into being "first things," from discovering to everyone's benefit what we're learning we can live without, so that we can live with each other in a more loving and honorable way.

There's just so much about this world that seems broken / can't fix the past or control what's to come / but for all we don't know / we know what matters most / are these moments right here in front of us / 'cause these moments are like treasures God puts in our hands / to spend any way that we choose / but if we spend them choosing to give love away / we'll gain the treasure we can never lose

from "Love Now"

Chapter 5

It's a Fight

We've got these friends, see, who—no lie, they're some of our favorite people in the world. We love and admire them so much. But there's something they do—or to be more exact, there's something they *don't* do—that we've never really understood.

They.

Don't.

Fight.

No fights. Ever.

"There was this one time," they admitted to us, as if it was killing them to confess it, "when we, um . . . we *a-l-m-o-s-t* had an argument." Something about a Christmas tree. Which probably tells you all you need to know, right there. Even their one and only "almost fight" smelled of fresh pine and mulled cider. But other than that—other than this ONE TIME—they could sit here and testify to you, right here today, that they have successfully made it through their several decades of marriage without succumbing to even a single shouting match.

And you know what? We believe them. We know them about as well as anyone does, and from what we've observed with our own eyes and ears from our many personal interactions with them, we've seen nothing to disprove the validity of what they're saying.

We're just saying we're not sure if we can be friends with them anymore.

Because what could they possibly have in common with *us*?

Fighting R Us.

Or at least it's *been* us, many many many many many times throughout our marriage. And if some of the same old patterns hold, another rousing fight could break out any minute, depending on what happens between now and whenever we get to the end of this writing day. Because even before we started in on this book you're reading now, we had already written the book on fighting: how to do it and how not to do it. And, we promise, you do not want to hear the audio version. Not of *that* book!

We admit to being fighters.

And we admit it's been a problem.

But we don't see much point here, in this book, in digging into all the whys and wherefores behind why we fight. We've got therapists for that. Or we've *had* therapists for that. Most of them have given up on us. Our goal right now is just to think out loud with you about how a couple like us, who love each other with all our hearts but possess our own history of not always getting along too well, can still be married after forty-plus years.

Because we're not so sure ourselves.

You can be excused for feeling a little whiplash, coming out of the last couple of chapters where we talked about the importance of surrendering, of seeing the other person's point of view, of giving in on things as a way of gaining the more important things.

And now we're into fighting?

Pick a lane, you guys.

Now please don't hear us making light of fighting. We're definitely not. We know how serious it can get, and we know how burdened you may feel about the fighting in your own home right now. We hope you also don't hear us recommending argument as being a central component of a good marriage. We're not saying that either. We sadly bear some serious battle scars on our hearts that we both would've done anything to avoid. (And believe us, we've tried!) A rainy day without a fight is better than a sunny day *with* one. But unless you're in the 0.00001 percentage of married couples like those friends of ours we talked about, who *never* fight, the battles will come. And you won't be able to laugh them off.

The question then is: What do you do when they happen? What do you make of them? What do you learn from them? And what do you do next? *After* them?

In case you've forgotten, because it's been a long time ago since we mentioned it, we were only nineteen and twenty-one when we got married. That's hardly even old enough to know what you're doing. And as we've already said as well, we had little preparation or insight into how drastically different we were from each other or what that would mean for us when life really got going. So our marriage lent itself to being contentious, right from the start.

It's not as though we *wanted* our relationship to be so high voltage. We felt terrible about it. We apologized and tried to fix it all the time. We made all-new promises on top of all the old promises. We worked superhard to keep it from catching fire again. Yet whatever we did or tried not to do, everything just kept going up in smoke. Again and again. Again and again.

So, as you hear us talking, understand you're listening to two people who have a long history of carrying around a lot of guilt together over this whole issue. We hated the fighting. We hated the feeling. And yet we kept returning to it, apparently not knowing or just willfully resisting any other way to handle ourselves when challenges kept coming up.

But looking back now over forty years, we sort of wonder if part of our problem wasn't a basic, faulty assumption of ours that we'd unwittingly brought along with us into marriage, kind of without saying so. Just this unrealistic expectation—this thought that every fight is one to be avoided, that every fight represents a failure of character, that we shouldn't have *any* fights or disagreements, *any* time. Not if we love each other.

Is that true?

We hope not. Because we *do* love each other fiercely, even though we do still have a lot of these "discussions." So maybe the best way to answer that question is not by pulling up the old scripts from all these fights of ours but by pulling back and seeing marriage, *all* marriages—our marriage, your marriage, everybody's marriage—in a much larger frame.

Most of us tend to focus our attention only on the parts of our marriage that are directly in front of us today, especially the parts that aren't going very well. Sure, we can easily drag the past into it also, but we treat the main battles in our marriage as if they're things that are primarily happening right *here.* Between *us.* Right *now.* In reality, though, our fights are not simply battles we've waged against each other (though it can often feel like we're always just battling each other) as much as they are battles in a larger war initiated a long time ago by our enemy, our common enemy.

In other words, marriage was a battle before we ever got here.

And that's important to remember. We'll talk about this more in a later chapter on all the wonderful things marriage is and stands for, the way God designed it. But underneath all of it—more than just the love story of two people coming together as husband and wife—is a sacred, holy story that's being told to the world. *Through* us. To our children, to other families. To our neighbors, to our fellow church members and coworkers, even to the "class of" whatever year we graduated high school. To everyone who knows us.

Marriage symbolizes the story of God's relationship with us. His love for us. His faithfulness to us. His grace toward us. His determination to fight for us, to keep coming for us, all because of His covenant with us. It's the story of promises kept, of our worst days redeemed. Of failing and falling but still being here. Never losing the courage of our hope.

It's the gospel. Marriage preaches the gospel. Not in a book or in a sermon but in a home, amid this beautiful but broken relationship that we two people share.

If that's *not* what it is, then try explaining why God, of all the metaphors or imagery He could've used, chose to describe His people as His "bride," and to describe our ultimate union with Christ as a "marriage" (Rev. 19:7).

Marriage demonstrates a gospel truth to the world. As told through real lives.

So the prospect of each of us having a united, functioning, thriving marriage (and having more marriages like it, all over the place) is an enormous threat to Satan's program. It enflames his anger and hatred toward God and, therefore, enflames his hostility toward us. It puts a big target on our backs. Anything he can do to divide us and break us down—to make the gospel story that our marriage is telling to others unattractive and undesirable—he's going to sign off on that in a heartbeat. "Steal and kill and destroy" is how the Bible characterizes his mission against us (John 10:10).

This is different, now, from what we've talked about earlier, about the *refining* aspects of marriage, where "iron sharpens iron" through some of our red-hot interactions (Prov. 27:17). That's where bits and pieces of old, ugly, unnecessary stuff start peeling off of us as the sparks start flying, as two stubborn wills collide. That's hard, and it hurts, but it's still positive because it's helping us grow. This honing and pruning, this shaving us down, this *sharpening* us as people and as a couple has a long-term purpose behind it, behind all this clashing. God is purifying us, perfecting us. He's working holiness into us—sanctifying us, remember?—even in letting us get all worked up.

But the battle coming *against* us, and against you, is coming with evil intent. And you're not the one who started it. When you were walking down the aisle, you were walking into a war zone. And you didn't even know it.

And the only thing worse than not being shocked by it *then* is being shocked by it *now*.

We've had daughters who in recent years were students at the University of Alabama. One of them was on the coed cheer team that performed during Alabama games. So, as a proud mom and dad, we've seen a lot of football from our seats at Bryant-Denney Stadium, along with other games at other places. Hopefully you never saw us on camera, because we liked being close to the student section where we could see our daughter better, and we kind of got into it, like people do around there.

We're talking big-time, big-boy, Southeastern Conference football action. The best of the best (unless you want to throw Ohio State in there, which would be fine with one of us). And yet one thing that's as true of a pickup game in the side yard as of a nationally televised playoff game on the big stage is that when one team is trying to move the ball and put points on the board, there's another bunch of players trying to keep them from doing it.

Not too many people would show up just to watch a team run plays without having anybody in different uniforms standing between the line of scrimmage and the goal line. (Except, okay, they probably *would* show up to watch it at Alabama.) But no one who's out there during a game is ever surprised to find opposing players working like mad to block them, tackle them, scheme against them, and prevent them from getting anywhere near the end zone. In fact, this other team and their coaching staff, all week long, have been back at headquarters, studying film, running practice drills, thinking up new and specific, even sneaky ways to make it as hard as they can possibly make it for your team to play good football. Their goal is to walk off this field, *your* field, as the winner to your loser on game day.

So. Expect a battle.

Because, what—did we think we would just come out here with our nice, shiny ball and our nice, shiny spouse, and every play that we dreamed up for how we wanted life to go would all just work? Without a hitch? "Gee, we were just wanting to go walking together and play catch together. So, what's with all this trash-talking us and chasing us and knocking us down and trying to steal our ball away from us?"

No fair.

No, we are *in* a battle. Your marriage *is* a battle, against a real enemy who is constantly whispering to you and making accusations—things about you, but more likely things about your wife or your husband. And he is never happier than when you're fighting and blaming each other with those same accusations.

So the sooner we can get to that place of saying, "Wait, *we* are not each other's enemy; *he* is our enemy," that's how much sooner we can see where most (or at least a lot) of our fighting is coming from.

Will it stop it all? Probably not. Hasn't completely stopped ours. The devil's campaign is a sinister one. He cloaks it in secrecy. It's easy to forget we're being played, being manipulated, that the stakes are so much higher than whatever subject is getting all the airtime in the house today. Between the two of us, we have frequently forgotten, in the heat of the moment, who we're really dealing with.

But here's the bottom line: It's not just you; it's not just her; it's not just him. You may or may not *have* a lot of fights, but you are *in* a fight whether you want to be or not. And this alone creates the environment for fighting, even when you're trying hard not to let it.

We've crawled on our hands and knees
/ through valleys cold and dark and

deep / sometimes not even sure if we /
could make it out alive / together
from "Together"

Now if anything we just wrote sounds like we're trying to make ourselves feel better for being such fighters, by palming off the responsibility for it to another source—okay, we'll accept that. Doesn't make it any less true that we're being actively opposed by enemy forces in dark and devilish places, but, yes, we should still be able to control ourselves when we feel the urge rising inside us for fighting back. Point taken.

What about *this*, though?

Shame enjoys attaching itself to anyplace where we know we've come up short. And when it comes to our struggles with fighting against each other, the two of us have given shame a lot to work with. When we think of how often we've been far less than gracious, godly, and patient in how we've expressed ourselves to each other—all the thousands of ways we've tried and failed at accommodating our differences—the shame of it could make us want to curl up in a ball and quit. Because we stink. We're losers. We've got nothing of value to offer anybody, the way we live around here. We should consider ourselves worthless for doing anything else, much less standing on stage, living behind this reputation for being such exemplary Christians. The most honest and proper thing for *us* to do, shame would tell us, is just to drop out of sight. Satan would love that too.

In fact, that's what's almost happened, more times than you might believe.

We've told this story in other places, but . . .

Steven: After Mary Beth wrote her book *Choosing to SEE,* in the aftermath of our losing Maria, we were approached with the notion of doing a seasonal tour that was more of a family affair. Caleb and Will would play in the band, I would sing, and—bonus prize—Mary Beth would speak. Kind of an inclusive concert experience. Call it "An Evening with the Chapmans" or something.

I thought it was a good idea. "Let's do it!" (Of course.)

That's me, holding up my half of the X-shape.

Mary Beth: And at first, I thought I'd be okay with it too. Well, I didn't think I'd be okay with it, but something inside me made me feel like it was an assignment I was supposed to fulfill. For a season. For a very short, very limited season.

We'd done something similar before, like when we went on *Larry King Live* together, and did other kinds of media interviews together after we lost Maria, wanting to testify how, even though we were broken and hurting terribly, we still believed God is good, that He is faithful.

Steven: But the closer we came to showtime, it ended up that the season we entered instead was one of our hottest, angriest, most volatile periods ever. It felt like the enemy was throwing everything he had at us to take us down. The onrush of emotions that had blindsided Mary Beth after going so deep into that writing project were spilling out with a fury. And here I was, not just catching them, but throwing them back at her in the form of new, now high-pressure expectations about this concert package I was trying to put together.

Mary Beth: I was so mad. Mad at Steven. Mad at God. Mad at this. Mad at everything. Mad at everybody.

Steven: I should've known. Why had I made such a commitment that I knew would end up this way? Whenever we take on something like this together (like this book, for instance), all hell breaks loose on us. We're just waiting for it to happen. But if there was ever a time when I thought there's no way our marriage is going to survive this, it was then. With all those concerts pending. With our homelife a disaster and our hearts in so much pain. And getting worse, not better. As embarrassing as I knew it was going to be, I had to pull the plug on it. Didn't I?

But in a moment of desperation, after all my praying about it and talking to our pastor about it and just beating myself to death over it—even as Mary Beth and I were feeling the waves of hopelessness taking us under—I called up the counselor we were seeing at the time and said,

"I'm doing the right thing, aren't I? By putting a stop to this?"

I mean, I could just see me standing up there, knowing what a lie this is, knowing how much pain and conflict were taking place offstage and behind the scenes. I could hear me singing "I Will Be Here," thinking the whole time about my wife being back there in the wings, listening to it, shaking her head, and saying, "If they only knew."

No. This wasn't happening.

It's the shame, see. From the fighting. It makes you want to quit.

But I'll never forget this friend saying to me, "Think about it this way, Steven: If you're up there, and you're there together, maybe that's enough—just that you're together. It doesn't mean everything's perfect or has been perfect. But for right now, can you just let it be enough? That you're together?"

Well, we'd ask the same question to you, if maybe we've caught you here on a day when shame is raining down on you. Maybe your home has been stuck in a hot-weather pattern for the past several months or years, and it's all you can do sometimes to keep pretending everything's okay when it's not. Can people tell? Are you afraid they'll find out? Would you rather just disappear than have to become known for what's really happening underneath?

Because shutting you down is the devil's stock-in-trade. Silencing your testimony. Making you believe you've got nothing worth sharing if you're not doing life nearly perfectly. But who ever said that's how it works? Where did we get that from? Just because your life and your marriage are not pretty all the way back into the background?

Are the two of you fighting? Is your family fighting? But are you still here together?

And can that just be enough? For now?

To keep showing up? Together?

We did the tour. We went ahead with it.

> **Mary Beth:** And on the last night, after I'd spoken for the last time, I leaned over to Steven, out of range of the microphone, kissed him lightly on the cheek, and said, "Can I please go home now?"

Yes, sweetheart. As long as we're going together.

Here we stand, here we are / with all our wounds and battle scars / from all the storms and all the wars we've weathered / together / we had no way of knowing when / we started way back there and then / how the road would twist and turn and bend / we just knew we belonged / together

from "Together"

All the fighting we've done reminds us that a couple can be together without really being "together" on everything. That's just a surprisingly big part of what marriage really is. Marriage does not mean you're always in 100 percent agreement. It's not perfect symmetry. You're dealing with so many different issues and problems every week, from daily decisions to future plans to private matters and family concerns and so much more, all wrapped up in your moods and your old hurts and your fresh worries and everything. You can't even get along with *yourself* half the time. What makes you think putting the two of you together is going to turn every conversation into a fruit smoothie?

The battle should not come as a shock. It really shouldn't. But God, in His grace and understanding, invites us to move our battle to another battlefield, to hand our battle back to Him, and to rephrase it in the language of prayer.

What if we did more of our fighting *there*? In prayer?

In a lot of ways, most of us just completely miss the point of what prayer is all about. We think it's got to be packaged and performed just right, that we have to be so incredibly careful and diplomatic with it, that before we pray we need to clear our throat and straighten the sofa pillows and be sure we're putting it into the kind of language God approves of, the kind of words that won't get us smited for saying them.

But this is not what you see in Scripture. Read the psalms sometime. You hear people there who are praying their anger, praying their tears, praying their sadness, praying their confusion. You don't hear God saying to them to hold your fire until you can calm down and get yourself under better control. You hear Him instead say to "pour out your hearts" before Him (Ps. 62:8). Just *bring it.* Whatever it is. Whatever you're right there in the middle of. Just shout it out. Let *Him* get involved in what you can't seem to get through. Drop your anchor *here,* right here in this craziest of storms. And feel yourself being pulled toward Him, and somehow being pulled toward each other too. It's like you're out there on the distant arms of that triangle, fighting each other, and yet you're being pulled closer together than you thought this fight would ever let you get, because in prayer you're being pulled closer to God.

One of our favorite Bible passages is the story of a king named Jehoshaphat. (Now *there's* a Bible name for you.) A couple of different enemy nations had joined forces to fight against him, and Scripture is honest enough to say he was scared about it. All the power seemed to be on the side of his opponent, and he didn't see a single way of surviving it. So he "resolved to seek the Lord," it says in 2 Chronicles 20:3. He brought all the people together into one place, stood there in front of them, and just prayed. He took the battle into prayer. He did his fighting in prayer. He said, in words that the two of us have probably prayed together a thousand times, "We do not know what to do, but we look to you" (2 Chron. 20:12).

That's a prayer. That's a prayer God loves. "We don't know what to do, God. We don't know where to go. We don't know how to get out of this. All we know to do is to cry out to You."

Many nights we have sat together in bed, after another bad argument, where the last thing either of us wanted to do was to invite God's presence around us. We were pretty sure He didn't want to see this, and we were absolutely sure we didn't want to be seen like this. We might only have been able to squeeze out one sentence of something you might call a prayer. But we prayed it anyway because He's said we can pray it, that we can "approach the throne of grace with boldness" at any time of night or day, "so that we may receive mercy and find grace to help us in time of need" (Heb. 4:16).

It's kind of the only thing we *can* do. To come at His invitation. And to count on prayer. To count on the fact that His Spirit is praying for us, interceding for us, groaning for us in heavenly places.

Because sometimes, down here on earth, it's all the fight we've got left.

We will fall on our knees / and fight like a warrior / we are the warriors on our knees / when we call on the name of the one who is conqueror / we're more than conquerors when we believe / the enemy trembles every time / 'cause he knows the battle isn't yours or mine / when we fall on our knees and fight / like a warrior

from "Warrior"

So, what do you do? About all the fighting? Again, we're not here to give ironclad answers or advice. We're just thinking through this thing: Why have we fought so much? And should we feel like the terrible people we sometimes think ourselves to be because of it?

We're still not sure.

But another counselor friend once shared a personal story with us that, even though it could seem kind of silly, we think it sheds light on this whole subject. It hints at another of the likely factors at play behind some of the frustrations all of us feel with each other in marriage.

He told of being out driving with his wife and another couple on their way to a restaurant for dinner. The man said he knew exactly where he was going, but his wife still felt responsible for being his GPS. She would point out that he needed to turn left at the next street, and not to forget to turn right at the stop sign after that one—you know, just generally being a passenger-seat driver. And he was hating this—*hating* it—hearing her tell him how to drive, making him appear small and henpecked in front of their friends.

Later that night, as he lay in bed, the counselor inside of him tried to process this encounter to help him understand why it had made him so furious. Why had it irritated him so much to be challenged or handheld or whatever he wanted to call this interaction with his wife?

Here's what he came up with. What if some of what he sensed boiling under his shirt collar that night was not all just pride at being told to do things he already knew how to do? What if it was more than just being petty, more than being offended at his wife for not trusting him and respecting his opinion? What if one of the triggers that ignites our short fuse toward our spouse (or toward anyone) is a *legitimate desire* for something all of our hearts are longing for? What if one of the reasons we get so frustrated with our imperfect wife or husband and with the imperfections in our relationship with them is because we're craving the *perfect relationship* we were made for enjoying with each other and with God, the way it was designed to be?

What if the reason we get mad is because we're wanting something good, something we were made for?

We are all so fallen. We are all so broken. We are all bent so low from having to deal with our own issues, not to mention the shortcomings of our mate. Is some of our fatigue with one another just a brokenhearted hunger for heaven, where none of these broken conditions will be part of our life anymore?

We're still not meaning to cop out on this. We're not looking for an available cabinet where we can file away our guilt and sinfulness under somebody else's initials. But what if, instead of becoming so distraught over the level of upset in our home, we could catch ourselves just long enough to say, "Hey, maybe this is us just longing for the beauty of our forever life with Jesus."

We want. We ache. We yearn. For more. And yet, except for God thankfully giving us a partial foretaste of it in the present, we cannot have everything He's promised us, not the way we will one day have it. And in the pain of not having it, sometimes our husband or our wife (bless his or her heart) is the closest and most convenient vessel for us to pour out our irritation about it, about not being able to experience *right now* all the things that comprise our future inheritance in Christ. We're not using it as an excuse for what we sometimes do and feel, but it might be part of the chemistry behind it. We can do the wrong things even when we're wanting the right things.

Okay. Have we solved anything? We don't know. These are just a few of the thoughts we've knocked around through the years in trying to come to grips with how volatile our relationship has often been. But maybe the best way to sum it all up is to say it like this: There's simply more to the fighting than meets the eye. There's a lot more wrapped up inside of it than just the current-events version that's screaming through the speakers today. The tone of the room right now may be intense, but it's occurring inside an eternal fight that's as old as the garden of Eden and will not be settled until that ancient, cursed serpent ultimately gets what's coming to him.

And we *cannot wait* for that.

In the meantime, maybe we just continue to battle, *within* this battle, for better understanding. We bear with each other's feelings and grievances in love, to the best of our ability. Which, because we're believers, means our ability is equal to the Holy Spirit's ability inside us.

And if it wasn't for God's mercy and his grace / there's no way we would be standing in this place / but because he has been faithful / every step along the way / here we are / together

from "Together"

Chapter 6

It's a Long Journey

Whew, glad we got that fighting chapter out of the way. But we knew we couldn't avoid talking about it. It's been such a heavy part of our relationship, and we're sure we're not the only ones who've struggled with it. And still struggle with it. It needed to be addressed, so . . .

You're welcome.

But still, we wish we hadn't been the fighters we've been. We wish we had been more patient, more understanding. Quicker with a hug and a smile than with a sharp word or a smart-aleck comment. Maybe if we hadn't always felt so pressed for time (nearly *all* the time), maybe then we wouldn't have felt like we couldn't wait long enough to listen, to do more than just emotionally react. Maybe we wouldn't have let false assumptions or selfish expectations back us into corners where the only thing we knew to do was to argue our way out of them.

It's been a journey, I guess is what we're saying—a journey we've been on, a journey we're still on.

But that's what life is. A journey. A long journey with God as well as with each other.

And it's important for us to remember this. Staying focused on this idea of *journey* has sure been helpful to us, especially on days when we're feeling the most disappointed by our failures, or when it seems like we're the farthest away from where we meant to be going, both as individuals and as a couple. Because if we're on a journey—and we are—a long, long journey—our lives are not limited to one glaring issue or to one painful season. On a journey, we are more than our regrets, more than the poor decisions we have made, more than just those isolated snapshots in time where the lighting was particularly bad.

The journey implies bigness. Lots of living space. And, because of it, lots of recovery space. It's not like the few directions on the front side of a recipe card, where one mistake or careless oversight can throw the whole dish off. Journey is more like a foldout poster world where even if we wander off the main road, even if we get separated deep in the woods, there's still a path that somehow circles us back together and works us around toward home. On a journey, we're given room to fail, yes, but also room to see failures redeemed, for living to tell the stories—the great adventures—of how God turned a highly impossible, highly imperfect stretch of our lives into a trophy moment for His grace that just keeps on being inspiring to us and to our family.

We can't say we've loved every day of our journey or the places it's taken us. It's sometimes come with a lot more of these adventures than we ever wanted. We can also tell you we haven't always been happy with ourselves, or with how we've complicated this journey of ours even further. But we love the truth of knowing our lives really do exist in a wide-open space with God, one that He patiently oversees and leads us through, and corrects us on, and helps us in. And just never gives up on us, no matter where it takes us or how difficult a traveler we become. As one of our favorite devotional writers, Oswald Chambers, says, "What we call the process, God calls the end,"[4] that for all its risks, regrets, and discomforts, the journey is still the best way—God's chosen way—for us to experience life. To experience *Him*. To learn who He is and discover who we are.

So wherever you find yourself on *your* journey today—whatever it looks like, whatever it feels like, whatever seems irreparably lost, or whatever is maybe going so well you think you've finally figured life out (always be careful when you think that)—we want to share with you a handful of what we hope are humble observations, things we didn't know about this journey when we first started it. If we had, our lives might've ended up looking significantly different. Simpler even. Less stressful. More peaceful. Who knows? And yet even with the scratched-and-dented journey we now call our daily life, we couldn't be any more loved and cared for by God. And had we done this journey any better, which we had every opportunity to do, we still would be no less dependent on Him for getting us to the next place in one piece.

We'll travel over mountains so high / we'll go through valleys below / still through it all / we'll find that this is the greatest journey that the human heart will ever see / the love of God will take us far / beyond our wildest dreams

from "The Great Adventure"

Steven: Mary Beth and I decided pretty fast, pretty early in our relationship, that we wanted to get married. We hadn't talked about it long, but we'd talked about it *enough* for me to know there really wasn't any mystery about what she'd say whenever I dropped to one knee and officially popped the question. And yet I was strangely a bundle of nerves the day I went to the mall in Paducah, Kentucky, to pick up the custom engagement ring I'd been anxiously waiting to arrive.

Don't overthink the word *custom* when you hear me say it. I had a friend back home who worked at Michaelson's jewelry store, and it is technically true that he custom-made the design and the setting I wanted for a diamond ring, that it didn't just come out of the display case. But I was still a poor, starving college student, even if I did have a bit of royalty money I'd made that spring from a song I'd written burning a hole in my pocket. Those few hundred dollars felt like a fortune to me. And isn't that what rich people do? Have their jewelry custom-made? (You are impressed, I can tell.)

So my money was already committed the day I drove into that old familiar parking lot. But what about *me*? Was *I*?

I *thought* I was. But even though the enneagrams paint me as this happy-go-lucky, fun-loving kind of free spirit, I promise you I can stress out with the best of them. I can suffer from terrible bouts of "paralysis by analysis," as my friend and pastor Scotty Smith calls it. I'm a lot more complicated than any old numbering system can figure out. I think everybody is. And in that moment, like a true worrywart, I was sensing the weight of what getting engaged to this woman really meant. To me, putting that ring on Mary Beth's finger was not only as good as walking down the aisle with her; it meant till-death-do-us-part going the distance with her.

And I panicked, there at the last minute. I didn't know if I was ready. I was afraid of what I was committing myself to do. Or maybe it was even more than that. I think we'd all be surprised at knowing just how much of what feels like fear or indecision to us at key moments in life is really part of the spiritual battle that's being waged around us and against us.

Over the years, as I've replayed the intense battle I remember experiencing that day, and now having lived forty years of what lay ahead of us at that point—in our marriage, in our family, in our ministry together, and in everything else that would flow from it—here's what I've come to believe: a very real enemy did not want us to marry.

I must've paced the full length of that mall for a solid hour or more. If you'd been following me on that big map in the middle, where it says, "You Are Here," I was everywhere. Everywhere but the jeweler's shop. Because I knew, the minute I crossed into that store and put that ring in my pocket, I was starting out on a journey. A

> big, long journey. And when you're right there at the mouth of it, at the entrance gate, with all of that walking to do in front of you, and you're daring to make a promise to it, to all of it, you don't know for sure if you can do it.

So there's an aspect of the journey that is just so fearful. What if you get out there and can't make it? Can't figure it out? What if you fail? What happens to the rest of your journey if you screw it up along the way? Is it all over then? Is there no way of ever recovering or making it up to everybody? No way to make it stop hurting? And no way to get it back on track? To work out a better ending?

Do you ever feel that way? Whether you're at the beginning of it or way out in the middle of it, life can sometimes just seem too big for you, too hard, especially if you're like the two of us, who in our own ways are determined to do everything right. And worried sick that we won't. And frustrated to death when we don't.

But sitting here today, we have a message we wish we could tell our younger selves (and maybe even our current selves), a message that might be timely for you as well, wherever you are. We're not saying life shouldn't be taken seriously. It should. Definitely, it should. But when you feel overwhelmed by the size and complexity of it, when all you feel is anxiety about where it's going and whether you're up to what it's asking of you, trust God more than you trust yourself. Let Him be the confidence that cancels out your lack of confidence. The bigness of the journey is not meant to frighten you but to bring freedom to you. And the beauty of it is that despite its size, your journey is as simple as your next step.

As the Bible says, "This is the way. Walk in it."

That's the verse that, over the years, God has repeatedly given us when we've just not known what to do, when we've felt outmatched by the accumulated pressures of overwork and over-worry. The words are from the Old Testament, from Isaiah, where he's telling Israel what they can expect from God as they journey forward with Him, in relationship with Him: "Whenever you turn to the right or to the left, your ears will hear this command behind you: 'This is the way. Walk in it'" (Isa. 30:21).

See, if you're not careful—or, maybe better to say, if you're *too* careful—the pressures of life can paralyze you. You'll come to a fork in the road where you're needing to make an important decision, and you'll freeze. You can't decide. Because you don't know what's right. You want to follow God's will, whatever it is for this situation, for whatever issue you're dealing with. But which way is He leading? And why can't you tell? And what do you do if you don't know? And what if in not knowing, you choose wrong?

It's scary. You can walk the mall over it.

But that's because you (and we) are often thinking too many steps ahead. The pace of the journey is not one of pacing the floor. It's just taking a first step. Then taking the next step. Then the next one. To the right. To the left. Now to the right. Now straight ahead.

That's how God leads us on this journey of trust, on this journey of relationship. "Your word is a lamp for my feet and a light on my path" (Ps. 119:105). Notice the brilliant metaphor the psalmist uses—"a lamp for my feet." The image he paints is more like a handheld lantern, not the high-intensity spotlight we might wish it was. The Lord doesn't lead by showing us every step from here to mile marker one thousand, lit up like a glowing highway. He does it by promising if we'll take that next step, He'll make sure it takes us somewhere.

If there's an ocean in front of you / you know what you've gotta do / take another step / and another step / maybe He'll turn the water into land / and maybe He'll take your hand and say / "Let's take a walk on the waves / will you trust Me either way / and take another step / take another step"

from "Take Another Step"

So pray and wait, sure. Listen. Get advice. Stay in the Word; be surrounded by the language of truth. But don't demand to see the whole layout before you move. The understood assumption of that verse from Isaiah 30 is that you're *moving*—right and left—and you're trusting the one who is guiding you. You're not walking the floor, you're walking in obedience—one step at a time—so that in this moment, you're experiencing the reality of following God's will. You're actively living the answer to that prayer you're asking. You want to know His will? Well, here it is. Take this next step of obedience with Him. Because, again, "what we call the process, God calls the end."

Most of us don't want a journey. We want a treasure map. We don't want today. We want tomorrow. We want the prize not the process. But, here, listen to Oswald Chambers again: "[God's] purpose is that I depend on Him and on His power now. If I can stay in the middle of the turmoil calm and unperplexed, that is the end of the purpose of God. God is not working toward a particular finish; His end is the process."[5]

The "end"—God's main goal, His primary objective—is how we respond in the "process."

Think of it in terms of what we Christians often refer to as our "calling." How does God *call* us to something? At what point do we feel *called*? And how do we ever gain clarity on exactly what this *calling* is?

For the two of us, whether it's been music or adoption or anything else we've sensed God leading us toward, the best we can tell you is that it's been a process. We didn't wake up one morning and were suddenly handed the GPS directions that the rest of our lives would be taking. Neither did you. But in the process of walking it out, God led us from one point to the next, and now here we are.

It would be funny (or terribly embarrassing) if we could somehow get up above the foldout poster version of our lives, if we could trace the spiritual route we chose to take from places like the Paducah mall to the life we're living today. What a tangle of twisted metal it would be. Surely, if God's will for our lives was basically one single grid, one linear path, stretching all the way from the beginning until now, we hopped off that train decades ago. If we were somehow supposed to decode it and do it perfectly, or else we were *out* of His will, we've been out of it for a long time. You couldn't get the knots out of this gigantic, crisscrossed ball of string we've made if you had a hundred years to do it.

But the journey makes all things new. The journey makes living in His will possible again. How? Because the journey keeps passing through a process called "today." And in that process, no matter what a mess we've made of it until now, we can still reach the "end" of what God has always had in mind for us.

That's a miracle. A hopeful miracle. A miracle of God's mercy. And every marriage needs that miracle. Every family depends on it. Ours wouldn't be here without it, there's not a doubt in the world, if God hadn't given us all this time to learn and grow and fail and forgive.

If He hadn't given us the journey.

Someday I will fly / and maybe then you will take me aside / and show me the bigger picture / but until I'm with you I'll be here / with a heart that is true / and a soul that's resting on your higher ways

from "Higher Ways"

Obviously the most challenging part of our journey as a couple and as a family has been our journey through grief, one we're still traveling. Some of the sharpness of it is gone, or has lessened at least, but we still sense it and feel it at every turn, often with unpredictable force. If ever we went through a season of life where it was truly one step in front of the other, where we really had no other choice than to fall forward, this was it.

So, where are we on that journey now? We're still in the process of it. And we always will be. We understand it better than we did, we think. We can say, as believers, that we've experienced a level of God's grace and help and the love of His people that we otherwise would never have known firsthand. And yet we can't say, as mere humans, that the cost has been worth those discoveries. We're still on journey on that. We're honest enough to say that.

We just want you to know we understand. We understand when journeys are upended and when the pain is unspeakable. We understand feeling sure you'll never smile or laugh again. We understand the insufficiency of answers sometimes. We understand the yearning for . . . I don't know, something settled. When nothing's settled.

But even *this* journey—this unsolvable journey—has left room for "this is the way" moments, opportunities for us to keep moving. To keep growing. To keep walking ahead.

Mary Beth: I've decided to share with you something extremely personal that I've never spoken or written about publicly before. I'm a little hesitant to commit it to paper even now because I'm still not completely sure what it means. But I feel like the Lord wants me to express it here, hoping it might resonate enough to help minister encouragement to you. It's somehow been encouraging to me.

It's a picture I see in my head. It's not a dream I had. I wouldn't call it a vision. It's just an illustrated thought that's come to me as I've wrestled with my own journey of grief and have tried to articulate it.

In this picture, I'm walking in a dense, mossy forest. I seem to be aware that these surroundings were scary to me at first, that at one time I was desperate about getting out of here. But the warm sun shining through the trees and the coolness their shade provides has made me feel comfortable enough to stay. It's okay now. Which is maybe why, when I can see the path that I'm walking is starting to lead me into a clearing, I'm a little anxious about it—anxious about being so close to the edge of this forest, oddly more anxious than when I was deep inside of it. I'm uneasy with the prospect of leaving it, if that's where this is headed.

But in front of me, in plain view through the thinning tree line, is a massive field of waving grass. Maybe wheat. Golden brown. Lush and beautiful, almost alive in the wind. And in the middle of it, there stands Maria! I can see her! She's standing on a huge, flat rock that's peeking up from the wheat field. I could run to her. She's right there!

But I don't. And I don't know why.

Part of me wants to go back into the forest. I once hated it there, but now I feel safer there. The forest of my grief, I suppose. So my first impulse, surprisingly, upon seeing Maria, is this initial check of hesitation. I can't believe I'm saying this, but in that moment, the forest has a stronger pull on me. It's become like a friend to me. A companion. I'm afraid to be outside of it.

I'd first run there when Maria died, having no other place to go. But in the years since, it has become sort of a shrine for me. My sadness was how I honored her. Grief was my debt to her. Walking out of it would feel like a betrayal of her.

So I'm torn now. If I head toward Maria, toward this daughter I want back, it will require me walking away from what I think is my sacred obligation to her. How can I do both and do what a mother should do?

But here's what is really unusual about this already unusual imagery. Between where I'm standing and Maria, on that same enormously strong rock, lies a calm and gorgeous but regally powerful lion. He is there with her. And now something changes in what I'm feeling. Knowing she is there with Him—with Jesus—that He is behind her, before her, and all around her, completely protecting her—is visibly more comforting to me at this point than the comfort of my grief.

The grieving me in this picture feels, yes, *comforted.* I feel wonderful really. I'm not angry, like I've sometimes been. I'm not in a hurry or feeling rushed to act, to do something, like I've often been.

I feel like maybe I *can* walk toward her, not away from her, even though I can't have her.

I can step out of the woods and into the light. And know I won't be risking failing her.

We think you know us well enough by now to know we're not people who believe you can patch up big problems with pretty answers. Nor would we ever try taking our own experience from our own journey and suggest it's the missing piece in your life, that if you'd only do what we've done, if you'd only learned what we've learned, you'd be in a much better place. We're all at *different* places. We're all walking the journey, but our journeys are not the same. We learn from each other, but we're not copies of each other.

It's just that inside this long journey—for all of us—it's easy to lose sight of reality. Of ultimate reality. The reality we can't see but that God says is true. The reality that Maria is *with* Jesus and that we as believers are going *to* Jesus. Part of the deception of living at street level in a sin-cursed world is that we can so easily confuse its happenings and activities as being the sum total of what's really going on.

And it's not.

We're not saying the losses are not real, whatever losses you're suffering today. Yes, they're real. The problems are real. The words that have been said, the things that have been broken . . . all real. Even the emotions they churn up inside you are real. But life with Christ means you can hold the realities of another world in balance with the things you're enduring in *this* world. Not as a delusion. Not as a mind game. But like C. S. Lewis said, "If I find in myself a desire which no experience in this world can satisfy, the most probable explanation is that I was made for another world."[6]

When we went through our intense season of loss, the grief blanketed us so heavily that we could hardly see anything else but sadness through it. That's normal. Unavoidable. But whatever

God intended by taking us on this journey—and, again, we're nowhere near understanding all the whys of it—He has used it over time to help us see other things, other realities, things we'd known and believed but had never truly laid our eyes on. Not clearly. Not *this* clearly.

For instance, He has given us a much deeper understanding of the power and hope in that little verse from John 11, "Jesus wept." As a child, it was the quick, on-the-spot answer you had ready when the Sunday school teacher asked if anyone had a Bible verse to share. You needed one that was short and sweet. But when you've wept at the level we've wept, when you've gone so far down into sadness and grief that you think sadness and grief are all you will ever feel or do, ever again, you truly begin to understand just how much goodness and sweetness is there in the picture of God's heart that He painted with those nine little letters: "Jesus wept."

If you remember the story, He had gone to the tomb of Lazarus. Surely He knew His purpose in going there was to raise His friend from the grave. By the end of that day, He was going to turn that whole situation completely upside down, to the amazement of everybody. What kind of demeanor, then, would you expect Him to show up with? Probably something like, "Don't worry, everybody. I know how to take care of this. I can do this. Just trust Me. Don't you trust Me? Can't you trust Me?" You'd think He would send off vibes of complete confidence, the kind that might make you feel ashamed for being "o, ye of little faith." What did He do instead, though?

"Jesus wept."

Lazarus's sisters were crying. Everybody who'd come there was crying. And Jesus, when they showed Him where the body of Lazarus had been laid, He started crying too. He entered into that moment with them, same as He enters into our moments. He sat with them in it. And stayed with them in it.

We'll never forget how, in those darkest moments of ours, the religious impulses inside us kept challenging us to buck up, to show some faith, to claim and stand on those promises that say, "Where, death, is your victory? Where, death, is your sting?" (1 Cor. 15:55). Those verses are obviously true and important and powerful. They hold up against every spiritual challenge. But we'll also never forget the deep release we felt when, in our weakness, in just our consuming sorrow, when we couldn't seem to summon up the energy to believe anything else, "Jesus wept" became like the only verse we could really claim—the biblical reality that says He weeps with those who weep, that in all our suffering, He suffers. And that it's okay just to pour out grief. Like *He* did.

The situation where Jesus found His friends that day, and where He found us that day, is not how life is supposed to be. He didn't make us to be separated from those we love. We weren't created for the purpose of being held captive by death. But He understands, far better than we do, what sin has done to us. He understands why the only prayers we can make sometimes are the guttural cries and screams of someone who doesn't have any other language to use. And once we'd seen the verse "Jesus wept" in this light, it was no longer the *shortest* verse in the Bible; it became for us the *longest* verse in the Bible—the longest of all possible expressions for just how much He understands us.

That's reality.

And as much as possible anymore, we want to see life through the lens of what God calls reality. To see it by faith, the way believers are meant to see. Living in His reality has sparked in us a new jolt of confidence. It's whittled away at so many of the yardsticks we once used for measuring our relationship with Him.

So in the middle of your journey—this walking-out-the-hard journey—work hard to believe He hasn't abandoned you to a hopeless, lonely walk. To untrustworthy promises. The only reason we've been exposed to untrue realities is because that's the deceptive world we live in. But that's not the world we're created for. And that's not the God who is holding on to us at the other end of our faith.

We can't tell you the next step to take. We're not sure we even know it for ourselves. But we do know if we're walking toward Him, we're always walking into what's real.

The veil that separates us now / is really nothing but a vapor / and on the other side we're finally gonna see and know / what was always true / that there was never even one heartbeat / when we weren't carried in our Father's arms / He's never taken his eyes off me and you / so for now will you walk with me / together we will keep remembering / to not be fooled by what we see / we've got everything to hope for / and nothing in this world to fear

from "Things Are Not as They Appear"

It is vital to know, when things look so bad, there is more reason to hope than to give up. It is crucial to remember, when you've failed at following, you can still find yourself back in God's will. In the process.

All of these realities, all of these adjustments to our perspectives, are blessings that come from having a long journey to live in. It's okay to need lots of room for letting God's grace do its work on you. That's actually what the journey is for.

But we can go you even one better than that: Your journey isn't even limited to your lifetime.

That's a lesson we discovered out on the 400 Mile Sale adventure. Do you remember us telling you about that? Our garage sale excursion? During that trip, just about at the time when we'd decided to break it off early and head home, we passed signs that said we were nearing the town of Glasgow, Kentucky, and remembered that's where Steven's grandfather, Virgil Chapman, is buried. He died before Steven was born, and we'd never been out to his grave. All any of us knew were the stories people had told about him.

And none of those stories were complimentary. The picture we have of Virgil Chapman's life is pieced together with a few not-so-great stories of his tumultuous journey and some heartfelt letters he wrote home while seeming to try to get his act together. This man, who appeared to start out with promise, abandoned his wife [Steven's grandmother] and their two boys when Steven's dad was just three years old, never to return. Dishonorably discharged from the Navy, he battled an alcohol addiction and ultimately lost the battle by the time Steven's dad was a teenager. Basically, he falls into the category of a drunk ne'er-do-well who left a wake of shame and embarrassment on the family name.

Finding his grave took some doing, even after we'd located the cemetery. But once we found it, we snapped a picture beside the simple little marker. It was as crude and uncared for as you'd expect for someone who died in his condition, with his reputation. But it clearly bore his name. For all his faults, he was an ancestral link in our family.

In the "Chapman" family.

The next morning, Sunday, we were back in church, and our pastor, Scotty Smith, preached a sermon that talked about some of the "ne'er-do-wells" who show up in Matthew 1 as being part of the family line of Jesus. Murderers, adulterers, prostitutes, serious sinners. Why would God choose to do it that way? Of all the bloodlines to keep pure, surely His plan for the Messiah would've avoided those kinds of shady neighborhoods. But He didn't. He worked through all sorts of sinful people to lay the groundwork for His Son to come. For sinful people.

And it got us to thinking: What about Virgil?

You'd have to imagine, in some of those moments when he was so miserable and alone, when not even a strong day of drinking could wash down the rot of his journey on earth, he thought it probably would've been better if he'd never existed. But if there hadn't been a Virgil Chapman, even with the choices he made, there wouldn't have been a Herb Chapman Sr. And without the choices made by Herb Chapman Sr., there wouldn't be a Steven Curtis Chapman either. Or our kids, including the three of them who were born half a world away. Or Show Hope, and all the families the Lord has blessed with the indescribable gift of a new life in their homes.

The journey each of us travels is just so much bigger than ourselves. God is writing a story, through both our best days and our worst days, that will live on beyond our physical time on the earth. There's obviously a great *responsibility* in that. We can also feel a lot of *regret* from that. But the *re-* words God is looking for—the part of this journey He specializes in the most—are the parts where He *redeems* and *restores* and *recreates* as we *repent* from our regrets and let Him *restart* what we thought was finished for sure. Not even the rank failures of others or the failures we've created ourselves can stop Him from making new things happen right here for each of us and for many years to come.

So let's do it, you want to? Let's pick up where our journeys have left off. We all can look back on unsavory moments and wish they'd never been here. And yet we're still here, with new choices in front of us today. And with room for Him to do the *remarkable.*

In us.

And for generations.

On this journey.

Then the world was broken / fallen and battered and scarred / You took the hopeless / the life wasted, ruined, and marred / and made it new / You make all things new / You make all things new / You redeem and You transform / You renew and You restore / You make all things new / You make all things new / and forever we will watch and worship You

from "All Things New"

Chapter 7

It's Ultimately One Decision

Imagine you're coming out of a restaurant where you've just been told the wait is thirty minutes. You're trying to decide whether to stay and tough it out or to go someplace else, hopefully someplace not quite so busy. Because who's got thirty minutes to kill like that?

Well, apparently, the old man and woman sitting alone on a park bench outside the door don't mind waiting. You hadn't noticed them at first, when you were walking in. But they caught your eye on the way out, as you were looking around to get a more accurate gauge for how many people were ahead of you in line.

And now you can't get these two old people out of your head.

Because, man, are they a picture. Sitting there. Turned toward each other. Classic wedding rings on their aging hands. A happy husband, a happy wife. After what looks to be so many years of life.

The expressions on their faces—the way she's grinning back at him as he's talking, until something he says must really tickle her because she leans forward in this cute little laugh, just as he reaches over and pats her knee. In reflex, she rests her own hand on his, until soon their fingers are interlaced, a lot like the smile lines creased at the corners of their eyes, as they keep talking back and forth. As they keep waiting their thirty minutes. As if they could go on like this forever, just enjoying each other's company.

It's beautiful. Adorable. Two people who not only still love each other but, from the looks of things, still *like* each other. A lot.

#Goals.

Get the picture?

All right, now hold that thought in your mind for a second while we pay a nod to a dear friend, Al Andrews, who first painted this "old couple on a park bench" imagery for us. Al for many years served a lot of people in the music business, particularly Christian musicians, by being a knowledgeable coach and a patient listener. And he once made an observation to us about this proverbial scene we've never forgotten.

Basically this. Yes, in one sense, this compatible husband and wife who seem to entertain each other so effortlessly are the quintessential model of marital nirvana. Utterly in love. No problems that overwhelm them, nothing they haven't solved or prepared themselves to deal with. Perfectly at peace and in sync with each other. Never a cross word or a cold shoulder. That's how they look. If we were to picture ourselves in that same seat at seventy, eighty, or whatever age is older enough than sixty to still seem *old* to us, it's what we all would want and wish for. The happy little couple who've gotten into their home stretch of life and are still enjoying the race. They've figured out the game.

And yet. Have they?

Or is it something *else* they've figured out?

See, Al was convinced if he could sit down in front of these two old lovebirds, and if he knew them well enough to ask the right kind of probing questions, he could get this happy little couple unhappy over something in a few minutes flat. Because in any couple's relationship, he said—even a couple as perfectly precious looking as this one seems to be—two or three hot-button issues are always sitting there that are not completely resolved between them.

But.

They've made a decision. To love each other and to bear with each other. They've said, in so many words, "I choose to do this journey with you, even though I'll always have things I wish I could change about you."

And as basic as it sounds, there is joy in just that. In that decision.

If they wanted to be full of contempt, the wood and the matches and the fuel source would be right there, easy to reach, ready to light. Just like with all the rest of us. No different. They'd be like just about every other old married couple, who couldn't go thirty minutes without bickering unless they were both agreeing with what the newspeople were saying on television. It's not as if the journey they've traveled has been without incident or is even without its own trouble right now. No one's life, no one's marriage, is always sweetness and light, and neither is theirs. But they've made a decision. They've *made* a *decision.* And they've long since buried the option of not sticking to it. They've said, like the song says . . .

Until one of us lays the other in
the arms of Jesus / I will be with
you / and you will be with me
from "Love and Learn"

And as far as we can tell, that's it. That's the secret. The secret to still being here. The secret that is so not a secret, just that it's not always what we want the secret to be.

So what Al would say is: Our perception of the park bench is a lie. The pain-free life, the perfectly pleasurable relationship we think it represents, doesn't exist. But the determination to keep a promise doesn't merely exist; it is indestructible. If forty-plus years of marriage has shown us anything—and we've given it forty million chances to prove us wrong—it's that nothing is bigger or meaner or stronger or more stubborn than this one decision.

The decision to still be here.

On a Monday / on a Tuesday / on a
Wednesday / all the way around to
Sunday / you've always got me / on the
good days / and the bad days / and the
mad days / the happy and the sad days
/ you've got me every day of my life
from "You've Got Me"

We knew going in, as we said, that writing this book was going to be a challenge for us. Not only are we a long way from being degreed experts on the subject of marriage, but our marriage has often been nothing to write home about, much less to write *everybody* about. We knew we were risking some fresh dings on our relationship every time we sat down to decide how much of our lives to expose like this and how best to say it. Our well-documented differences (or at least we've well documented them for you now) simply do not lend themselves to this kind of collaboration, we can guarantee you that.

But here's the challenge that's dogged us even more than that one. How can we talk about what we've found to be the main ingredients of a *Still Here* marriage, knowing someone who is reading these words right now is on the other side of a marriage that isn't here anymore?

Few things can more quickly trigger a person's regret reflex than the history they've had as a wife, a husband, or a parent. And don't we know it. We've had the same reaction any time we've read other books on marriage and family. "Well, we sure messed *that* up, didn't we? That'd been nice to know twenty years ago, when we could've done something about it."

But, hey, if you're hearing whispers of shame right now, they are not coming from the Holy Spirit. It's possible you're hearing them in the sound of your own voice, but trust us, they are the whispers of the enemy. They are the ugly catcalls of the accuser. And we are all susceptible to them. The two of us hear them all the time. But instead of allowing them to keep playing, instead of letting him amp them up, maybe it'd be a good idea for you to close this book for a second or two and let the Spirit Himself speak to you. Of newness. Of new beginnings. Of redemption.

Of how the "God of hope" can "fill you with all joy and peace as you believe" (Rom. 15:13). We all survive on nothing else than the possibilities of grace, new every morning. We can't go back and undo old things. We can only move forward and believe Him for new things. The only thing any of us has is today.

So let's start there.

We talked in the last chapter about the importance of living in reality. And according to what Jesus said about reality, the way a person finds true life is by choosing to "deny himself, take up his cross daily, and follow me" (Luke 9:23). Now if that's just for Sunday school or for Sunday sermons, we can all nod to one another nicely and say we've been to church. But these words of Jesus are *not* just for Sunday. They're for the Monday, Tuesday, Wednesday kind of life that happens in your home and in our home. On the daily.

And yet being the selfish people we are, we don't like where this denying of ourselves and taking up our cross is going, this following the example of the One who laid it all down for us. Except that the future of our marriage depends on it.

Which means, we've got a decision to make. Am I dead set on being sure I get what I want and what I think I deserve out of this relationship? Am I determined that my spouse sees things the way I want him or her to see them, or else he/she has not heard the last of it? Am I going to have my shot at the life I always envisioned for myself, even if the only way I see it happening is for me not to be staying with you? And would anybody else, given the set of circumstances I'm living in, not do the same thing? If they could? How can I expect to put up with this—with you—and still be content?

This is a hard conversation to have with yourself, about you and your marriage, about you and your spouse. Know how we know? Because we've had it. Many times. But the hard things we've needed to tell ourselves, and the hard things we've sometimes felt led to say to a lot of other people as well, usually ends with this: "What if I just laid it all down? What if I denied myself what I want? And what if, the next time I find myself feeling this way, I laid it down again? What if it had to be me every time? Would I be willing to do that?"

True confession: We have *not* been willing, on tons of real-life occasions, to do what those questions are asking. But we have learned, every time we're at odds with each other, it's because one of us (if not both of us) is bucking the cost of living in that reality, where laying it down is the cost of doing long-term life together.

Yeah, but you don't understand.

Right, we've said that too. How nobody understands. How nobody's got it as bad as we do. How nobody could be content if they were dealing with the level of strain we're up against or the sacrifices we're having to make to keep this marriage going.

If you wouldn't mind us using an extremely personal event as an example, we'd tell you we can think of no tragedy more unbearable than the one we lived through when we lost Maria. And it can still feel that way. Unbearable. But are we the only ones who've ever lost a child in an awful way? Are children's hospitals not filled today with moms and dads sitting at the bedsides of the kids they love, watching them suffer through aggressive illnesses that seem so out of proportion to their young souls and bodies? Watching their pain drag out over long, exhausting months and years? Our ordeal has been bad enough, by any metric. But still, we haven't been made to endure a hardship worse than what anybody else has ever been through. What we've been through has been survived before. By many others.

And the same logic, the same reality, goes for every ordinary daily difficulty that each of us faces in life, in marriage, in parenting, in whatever. We are not being picked on or picked out for what feels like a unique level of intolerable living conditions. A lot of other people we know and don't know are going through the same and worse. We're not the only ones.

But one decision still applies to all of those difficulties, to all of us.

Am I willing to stay through this? Or not.

I know it's going to take a lifetime / to answer
this prayer I pray / but that's okay / 'cause
I've given You and her my lifetime anyway
from "How Do I Love Her"

It never escapes us that "I Will Be Here" is the song our marriage is known for. Perhaps that's why we've sometimes thought, *Instead of music, we should've gone into the casino business or something, where at least we'd have been no threat to the enemy's operation.* Then maybe he'd have left us mostly alone, and maybe it wouldn't have been so tough to "Be Here." But between our deeply contrasting chemistry and our pull to keep following through on what we thought the Lord had called us to do, even if it pulled us apart, we dug in there and did the best we could.

And we fought, and fought, and fought to make it stick. We've told you about that.

We are aware of how often the marriages of people who are creative artists and public figures don't survive the similar tensions we've experienced in spades in our lives. We're not comparing, and we're certainly not complaining, but we're also not superhuman. So, yeah, we've had our own times when we've thought maybe it *would* be better for the kids if the two of us weren't together. They probably wondered the same thing about us themselves as they got older, how everybody really might be better off that way. Us *and* them. They saw families of their friends whose parents had divorced, where things seemed to be working out all right, where everybody appeared to be a whole lot happier and less agitated, now that the fighting was no longer confined to their common living areas.

It can start to make sense.

And you can start being talked into it. People will say you're finally being brave enough to take care of yourself, that you're learning the lesson of the airplane oxygen mask, that the best way for you to love the people around you well is to make sure, first of all, that you're breathing well yourself. It's not hard to find a counselor, even among the ones who advertise themselves as "Christian" counselors, to encourage you right out of your marriage. Out of the *decision* you once made—both of you—to live your promise through to the end.

The facts are the facts. We get that. The reasons are always around us for making different decisions now than we did then, for putting new conditions on our old vows. But the truth is the truth: We live in an environment that coddles us in our facts and then reasons us into selfishness. What we need are not more excuses for feeling better about focusing on ourselves, our needs, our wants, our sins, our everything. We need more people—sinners like us—feeling motivated to follow through on our decisions, *making* the decision to *stick* to our decisions. Even when it's hard.

And, man, is it hard. Sometimes impossibly hard. It's hard to say, hard to do. Hard to lay ourselves down, take a hard look at the situation, and determine we are hardly the one who deserves an easy way out of this. Are we really seeing ourselves in an honest light when we look at this other person in our marriage and conclude *they're* the reason we can't live this way anymore?

The statistics say we're not looking at hard facts when we say that. Just for reference, roughly 40 percent of first marriages end in divorce. This number has actually come down a bit from the 50 percent we commonly heard throughout the last half century. But here's the surprising stat, given how confidently an unhappy marriage partner thinks about their situation, how convinced they've become that a change of surroundings would make them so much happier. (Be honest now, you've thought it.) The divorce rate for second marriages is *60* percent. And for third marriages, more than *70* percent.[7]

Now that's interesting. We realize numbers, too, can be deceiving. Many second and third marriages are successful. But what does it mean when, on average, if you take a person from one marriage and you place them in another, the likelihood that they'll struggle in that marriage as well is not *less*; it's *greater*?

Again, the only reason we feel passionate enough to write about this commitment to stay together is because we want to be both a strong and gentle voice of encouragement to you in whatever situation you find yourself (and because we need to hear it again ourselves). But these figures tell us something. They tell *all* of us something, whether we've been married for years or are still getting used to sharing a bathroom sink with this person. They tell us the issue with seeing our marriages through to the finish is in most cases a *me* problem, not a *you* problem. If one person—namely, me—would see what my resistance to denying myself is doing to both of us, all the trends on those number lines would start to shrink in size. And our homes would be places where promises are kept and where people feel solid. For a lifetime.

We'd be the couple on that park bench.

And we'd have a lot better story to tell.

A story of not quitting. A story of not giving up. A story of God giving us room on our journey for always taking another step, even through the hardest slog of it—room for hearing that voice behind us, telling us, "This is the way. Walk in it." He walked us through hell, but in the end, check it out: We were walking together.

Don't give up on that being your story.

It could so easily not be *our* story. And we've got no humble brag for why it isn't. It's the grace and the mercy and the faithfulness of God. It's whatever He wired into us, and what we've tried to impress on our kids from an early age: You don't quit. You keep pushing. You keep trying to learn. You stubbornly fight on, fighting anything that would keep you from staying here.

Mary Beth: You know, Steven recorded an album in the early 2000s, called *All About Love*. He wrote ten new songs of commitment for it, and it's worth looking up if you've never listened to it. I was given the important title of being executive producer for the project, which basically meant I got to pick the songs that went on it, including a couple he *didn't* write but that I just wanted him to cut. Like the "500 Miles" song you may have heard us butchering on Instagram. So there.

But—how can I say this?—the *All About Love* CD or digital stream or whatever it is now is not just my husband singing a record of love songs. This man has decided—no doubt in my mind, doesn't matter what happens—he is going to keep showing up. Like a bad penny. (No, like a *good* penny, a nice and shiny penny that's been found.) Even when I maybe don't want him there, he is going to be *right there*.

Listen, I can dish it out. I've given him a lot of reasons for not wanting to hang in there. Like the lady on the park bench, if she was being honest, I still want him to change for me, to change the speed he travels at, to give me more control over what our calendar is going to look and feel like this coming year. But, end of the day, whatever it costs him, he is not going anywhere. He has solidified that for me.

So, when I hear him sing that song, the "I Will Be Here" song—even though (news flash!) Steven Curtis Chapman's wife doesn't listen to music very often—I know he's going to be here. And I hope he's just as confident that I'll be here for him too, right beside him.

Steven: You know I am.

Mary Beth: But if you're a husband and you're reading, I just want you to hear what this means to your wife, because I think it's way too unusual, and it makes me sad when I think about the people I know who can't say this. There's a comfort that comes from knowing I have the freedom to push hard against him when I'm frustrated. Even in laying it down, I can let it be known what I'm experiencing. I don't have to sit on my feelings and tap dance around issues that are important to me. It won't cost me my marriage, or even the future happiness in my marriage, if I tell him honestly what I think. His decision—*our* decision—helps us to live like that.

I've been bragging on him here, because he's legitimately earned it, but it's sometimes hard to get his full attention and be sure my thoughts are being heard. Know what I mean, ladies? With *your* husband? But the strength it gives to me, knowing I cannot push him away, that he will still be there when we get on the other side of this, is more freeing and life-giving than I can describe.

Steven: And I feel the same way. I mean, Mary Beth has laid it down for me. My life drives her crazy. I know it. She wants it predictable and manageable, seemingly controllable, and I am so aware of how often all I seem to do, in her eyes, is drop another straw into the drink and stir everything up into a big bubbly whirlwind.

> But she has never given up on me. She's never let go of me.
>
> And I've pushed *her* hard too. Even in trying my best to make every decision in the context of how it will impact her peace and her happiness and joy and our family, I know how often I end up delaying her from settling into some of the desires that matter to her.
>
> Yet through it all, I look across the table, and there she is. My beautiful, brown-eyed college sweetheart. She's been through so much, she's fought so hard, and she's still there. She's still here. And, thank God, I know she's not going anywhere.

We've just decided that's what we're going to do and be for each other. We wish we had a snappier way of saying it or a bunch of party-game exercises you could try at home that would produce the same results. But maybe the most underreported reason we as a society have such a hard time keeping our marriage vows is because it's really just a matter of keeping them. As unsensational as that. Not much of a headline there. "To have and to hold from this day forward." There's not a trick to doing that. There's just a commitment to it.

A decision. One decision.

I know sometimes I let you down / but I won't let you go / we'll always be together

from "Go There with You"

Our kids call it the "Chapman energy." We laugh when we hear it, and maybe we shouldn't have crammed them so full with it, but we Chapmans are just a determined bunch. Once we're in, we are ALL IN. We see it in Emily, in her sweet-hearted tenacity, in how she puts her deep, thoughtful, convicted passion for excellence behind everything she does. We see it in Caleb and Will and their incessant dedication to their music craft and to the many little details that go along with it, to the things they're writing and working on. We see it in Shaoey, in the amazing effort she poured into not one but two streams of study in college and how she continues to pull the best from herself as she branches forward into life. We see it in Stevey Joy, how this tiny little human can exude so much light and be so athletic and adorable, how she can be so firmly grounded and yet turn these dazzling somersaults from twenty feet in the air.

We're even starting to see peeks of it, of the Chapman energy, in our grandkids. Lord, help them. And their parents.

Sometimes we sit back and watch how our now grown children just habitually seem to push past their normal limits, how they don't take no for an answer, how they ask hard questions and do hard things. And we think, *My goodness, did we do this to them?*

Maybe we did. It's not like we wanted any of them to get hurt, but we do want them to be people who, once they've committed to something, once they've said they're going to do it, that they do what it takes to follow through on it. They dig deep and they press on. We're so proud of them for that.

But it doesn't matter how determined you are, or how young and upbeat you are: there are days when you don't feel it. And by the time you add more age to the situation, like the sixties we're feeling now, even more of those days tend to show up in a calendar year. There are some mornings, there are some subjects, there are some afternoons where you've already needed about double your normal caffeine intake just to tackle what you already knew was on your plate. But let your spouse lob in one extra pushy or irritating complaint or demand, with no sensitivity to cushion it—let them add it to your stack at the worst possible time, without seeming to consider how it affects the plans you'd already made—and now you're officially over it.

Let's see how well your one-decision mentality serves you now.

So we hope, in talking about the power of "one decision," that we haven't come off sounding too simplistic. Too stoic. Too Chapman energetic. We've all done enough resolution-making in our lives to know we're traditionally deficient in that department. We need more than what's inside of us if we expect to do what marriage calls us to do.

But remember, we serve the ultimate Promise Keeper. And He is able to help us do all things—"all things through him who strengthens me" (Phil. 4:13)—even when we're having the hardest time keeping the promises we've made.

We are in that relationship with Him like we described a little earlier, where we know He's not going anywhere. We can get upset about what the cost of following Him is demanding of us. We can feel sorry for ourselves because the burdens we're having to carry seem like more than we're able to handle, whether in marriage or in other areas of life. We can even deliberately choose to react in rebellion to Him and to what He says is best for us, or to give Him the silent treatment—a prayerless, indifferent, dismissive attitude. But He has proven Himself to us. He sent Jesus to the cross for us. He drew us to Him and made us one of His kids. He can take it when we struggle and stumble, when we fume and fail and fritter out—just like parents do with their own children—because He's made a decision never to let go of us.

So on those days when our Chapman energy is running low, or on those days in your own life when you're just about ready to give up, we as the children of our heavenly Father are not left to the gritting of our own teeth. We can run to Him. We can beg for strength. We can receive His forgiveness. We can start over. Yeah, we can *make the decision* to start over. To trust Him for what's too big for us. To love when we don't feel like loving. To give when we don't feel like giving. To latch onto His unbreakable promise that He will help us keep our promises.

So join us back at the park bench for a second. The mystique of it is so misleading. It makes us feel, just looking at it, what everybody else feels. That we are so not there. That our marriage has too many problems, too many places where we can't get along, where we just will not bend, where we're pretty sure we've lost all hope for having the marriage we meant to have. That it's never going to be as beautiful as this one. As beautiful as it could've been.

But what the park bench might actually do, if we know what we're looking for, is to remind us the goal is possibly a lot closer than we thought. It doesn't require us to figure out how to untangle all the complexities that have been rankling us for years as a couple. It doesn't require us to make up for all the mistakes that in many ways cannot be satisfactorily undone. It doesn't require us to turn ourselves overnight into the kind of spouse, the kind of person, we always thought we would be. Maybe it can just start with one decision.

Could you and your mate just decide today that you're not going anywhere? Just take that word, the quitting word, off the table? Retire it from your vocabulary? One decision can do a lot.

Will removing it from the conversation make all your problems disappear? No. But remember, there are problems on the park bench too, just like there are problems that remain at our house, just about anywhere we sit. Yet for all of these problems inside, there's one potential problem we've deliberately shown the door. And it's made a huge difference. This single decision has gotten us through stuff we didn't think we could get beyond.

We're not always sitting pretty. But at least we're sitting together.

The music will play / and I'll hold you close / and I won't let go / even when our steps grow weak and slow / still I'll take your hand and hold you close to me / and we will dance

from "We Will Dance"

Chapter 8

It's Lots of Grace

You can make all the music in the world, but there's nothing like the old hymns. They speak with a depth and a glory that is hard to replicate or recapture. Like *this* old hymn, for example:

There's a wideness in God's mercy
Like the wideness of the sea;
There's a kindness in His justice
That is more than liberty.

There is no place where earth's sorrows
Are more felt than up in Heaven;
There is no place where earth's failings
Have such kindly judgment given.[8]

"There's a Wideness in God's Mercy." Not many modern songwriters would think to put it like that. But what a great lyric to carry around in your thoughts and in your soul every day, when you think about the mercy and the grace of God—what it is and how He wants us to experience it. It has an infinite "wideness" to it, "like the wideness of the sea." Even wider, how it just goes on and on and on . . .

For the love of God is broader
Than the measure of our mind;
And the heart of the Eternal
Is most wonderfully kind.[9]

For us, probably our most vivid experiences with it, with the wideness and broadness of who God is and how He operates, have occurred in some of the most visually heartbreaking places on earth. Like, in the primitive jungles of Ecuador, worshipping with a tribe that once took the lives of missionaries trying to tell them about the love of Jesus, or in the impoverished villages of Uganda, when you hear the voices of little children singing. You look around at conditions that appear as God-forsaken as anything you've ever seen, and yet rising up out of this hard-packed ground of need and hunger and suffering and danger come these tiny songs of praise. Because He's there. In that. In them. By His grace.

Or in death-row cellblocks where you expect to find the deepest darkness and hopelessness, and yet you look into the eyes there of a man God has radically set free from the prison of his sins. You came to encourage *him*—people like *them*—but he can't stop encouraging *you*. This murderer, who says he fully deserves the punishment he's getting, is challenging you not to lose heart, not to lose faith, to go out there and grab every chance you can get for telling people about what the love of Jesus can do. Because you've seen it in here. The last place you'd *ever* expect to see it. How do you explain that?

God's grace.

Because it's true. Nowhere and no one is outside of His saving reach. Wherever we live, we live by the grace of God. All of us. Whoever we are, however accomplished or hardworking we think ourselves to be, we deserve the same judgment as everybody else. And yet whatever we've done or not done, in all the millions of ways we've failed Him, God's grace is enough for us. By His grace we are saved, "to the uttermost" (Heb. 7:25 ESV).

Grace is another one of those ultimate realities we are made for living in. And it's good to review this gospel reality often, because it keeps us continually reminded about giving thanks to Him for His gift of new life to us in Christ. But it is so much wider, so much broader than even that. Grace, when we truly believe it—grace, if we'll just surrender ourselves to it and receive it—can drive the daily rhythm of every relationship in our home. Grace, when it's coming out of us as freely as it's coming into us, can help us establish a new flow and heartbeat to all the dynamics of our marriage. We all need what grace gives.

But . . .

> But we make His love too narrow
> By false limits of our own;
> And we magnify His strictness
> With a zeal He will not own.[10]

See, here's a problem. We know what the Bible says. We know what we're supposed to believe, how Jesus gave Himself for us on the cross, how we've been declared righteous before God by the purity of His sacrifice. We even know His grace is what continues to keep us going now as believers, that we can do "nothing" without relying on Him every day (John 15:5), that even in this moment, "if we confess our sins, he is faithful and righteous to forgive us our sins and to cleanse us from all unrighteousness" (1 John 1:9). But we have such a hard time seeing it, don't we?—seeing ourselves as being unconditionally loved and accepted by Him. Surely He can't really feel that way about us. With what He knows about us.

If you were raised old-school like we were, you knew better than to get too comfortable in your walk with God. They preached grace at church to get wicked sinners to walk the aisle to Jesus, but once you were saved and supposedly able to figure it out on your own from there, grace wasn't so much a part of the discussion anymore.

Somewhere out there was a line, God's last nerve, the limit to the types and the number of sins you could commit before you'd pushed your luck too far. And you never knew how close to the margins you were already playing it. You just knew you'd done and thought a lot of things you shouldn't and that it wouldn't take much more of a misstep before—[loud buzzer audio here]—the trapdoor might just open up, right out from underneath you.

So even though you'd surrendered your life to Jesus to invite Him into your heart, you had to work hard to keep Him there. That was your part of the deal. It was a "God helps those who help themselves" kind of thing. And because you couldn't do it with everyday consistency, it led to a lot of guilt. A lot of distance and fakeness and religious hypocrisy. A lot of beating yourself up, thinking you'd lost whatever right you used to have to "approach the throne of grace with boldness," because you weren't sure what kind of reception you'd get now if you did. The safer route, it seemed, was just not to get too close. Maybe He wouldn't notice.

And that's how a bunch of us spend much of our days. Not enjoying His love for us but calling ourselves angry, ugly names. Not sensing His favor toward us but only our inner critic's dissatisfaction with us, our running soundtrack of shame and self-disgust. We want *Him*; we just don't know if He wants the real *us*. And if we ever do get on enough of a steady streak where we think maybe we've earned His smile of acceptance and can feel a bit more at ease around Him, we eventually lose our balance again and revert to being undependable: "What's the matter with me?"

Yes, what's the matter with us? The "matter with us" is that we don't really believe in His grace. And if we don't really believe in His grace—His grace for *us*—we can't really be instruments of His love and grace to others.

Like to the other person in our marriage.

This is what I'm sure of / I can only show love / when I really know how loved I am / when it overtakes me, then it animates me / flowing from my heart into my hands / so I'm praying, Father, help my heart believe / that right now You're singing over me / and fill me up with Your love

from "Love Take Me Over"

The two of us are not people who go easy on ourselves. One drawback from having the Chapman energy is that you always think you could've done something better. Maybe, maybe, you can allow yourself room to feel sort of good about what you did. Maybe. But underneath, you're left questioning two or three places where you think you came up a little short. Maybe a lot short.

It sets us up for having a disconnect. On the one hand, we are utterly bought in, both mentally and spiritually, to this idea of being forgiven and forgiving. But to be honest, our personal tendency toward ourselves is to be *un*forgiving. And unrelenting.

And that is a recipe for unhealthy regret, for all the "should-have-beens and not-yets," the ones we "keep on dragging around." Steven has sung about that, in "The Long Way Home," how "I can hardly wait till the day I get to lay them all down."

Regret. Just the sound of that word is like a jab in your side—what could have been, what should have been, if you hadn't done that, or hadn't been like that, or hadn't become like that. It's a vicious cycle of what-ifs and why-did-yous. And yet they keep drawing you in. You think if you keep chasing them around the track enough times, you'll finally spot a weakness in their arguments. You'll uncover an insight that gives you a better answer for why you did it, or at least a justifiable alibi that you can bear to live with. But the only thing that chasing your regrets ends up doing is funneling you deeper into frustration and disappointment. And from down in that pit, it's too dark to see how grace can possibly come in and pull you out.

It's made us wonder, on those days when we're being the hardest and most unforgiving on ourselves, *Isn't there any other way to look at regrets?*

We've told you we have a great affinity for those *re-* words. They're recalibrating to us. Words like redemption, restoration, renewal, recreation. Think of that last word for a second: *recreation*. We were brought up to think recreation was for wimps. Recreation was synonymous with goofing off, with wasting time. Just a lazy excuse for not working. People who loved their recreation too much were irresponsible. Do-nothings. Slackers. But if you poke into that word a little more, you see recreation is a healthy, God-given investment in our "*re*-creation." Rest and play and exercise are not wastes of our time; they are activities that breathe fresh life into us. They re-create us.

Well, what about *regret*? Is there any redeeming that word too?

According to the dictionary, *regret* appears to come from an ancient root that means "to weep." Which, of course, makes a lot of sense. But here's what we find intriguing. The part of the word that means "to weep"—*greter*—is born of the same word family that gives us our English word *greet*. A happy word.

Hmm.

So forgive us for taking a little license with all of this, but see if it might not make a viable point. What if, the next time regret showed up heavy on your doorstep, you didn't treat it like a robber coming to steal your peace and joy? What if, you know, you *greeted* it differently? What if it was less like opening the door to a haunted house on Halloween and more like opening the door to your family on Thanksgiving?

Because, hey, when we think back on some of our failures as a family, on our not-so-stellar parenting moments with our kids, some of whom show up here now (like at Thanksgiving) with their spouses and their own kids, we can feel those waves of regret come rolling in. Man, do we wish we could go back and do a lot of it over. Do a lot of it better.

But is any family picture-perfect? After all these years of up close, in-home interaction, can any family, can any parent, claim to be completely free of regrets? When we pull in one of our grown children today for a close hug and a kiss on the head, we know they are not the perfectly pristine result of our perfectly pristine parenting. They are living, breathing testimonies to the God who worked through our stumbling-around failures and has wrought beauty out of our brokenness.

So let's talk reality here, God's ultimate reality. Do you know why the Lord gives us grace? Do you know why He forgives the sins of His children? Not just so we can escape hell when we die, although that's good for *us.* He does it primarily to bring glory to *Him,* so that He can show us off as miracles of His mercy. Paul said it like this: "So that in the coming ages he might display the immeasurable riches of his grace through his kindness to us in Christ Jesus" (Eph. 2:7).

God is not ashamed of us, even when we fail. He's not shaking His head because of what we did; He's bragging on what His *grace* did. And is still doing. And keeps doing, even with our grimmest and grimiest regrets. It's His grace, not His law, that transforms us into people who *want* to obey Him.

And so the taller and gnarlier our pile of regrets—this is unbelievable—that's how many more opportunities He can take for showing the world the amazingness of His grace. Our regrets are not meant for rehashing us into despair but for being repurposed through our repentance, redeemed by His grace, so that we can experience life with Him "without regret" (2 Cor. 7:10).

They're not dead ends; they are open doors.

Maybe we should stop regretting them and start regreeting them.

If the truth was known and a light was shone
/ on every hidden part of my soul / most
would turn away / shake their heads and
say / "He still has such a long way to go" /
if the truth was known you'd see / that the
only good in me / is Jesus / oh, it's Jesus

If the walls could speak of the times I've
been weak / when everybody thought I
was strong / could I show my face / if it
weren't for the grace / of the One who's
known the truth all along / if the walls
could speak they'd say / that my only hope
is the grace / of Jesus / the grace of Jesus

But, oh, the goodness and the grace in Him
/ He takes it all and makes it mine / and
causes His light in me to shine / and He loves
me with a love that never ends / just as I
am / not as I do / could this be real / could
this be true / this could only be a miracle
/ this could only be the miracle of mercy

from "Miracle of Mercy"

Grace is such an essential. It's really the ultimate essential in being able to believe in a world where we and the God of the universe can genuinely relate to each other. Our relationship with Him simply doesn't exist without grace. God's grace. "Grace that is greater than all our sin," as another great old hymn says it. Grace is at the heart of the gospel, undeserved in every definition of the word.

And only in light of God's grace—what we could maybe call big-G grace—can we even begin to express a small-g version of His grace toward others. You can't really talk about showing more grace to your wife or husband, to your kids and your grandkids, until you're truly walking in the fact of how God has shown His grace to you.

And we've needed (and continue to need) a lot of learning on that.

For us, on most days, it starts with just the normal, ordinary, up-every-morning aspects of life. That's where grace, over time, has gradually remade us into the shape of that triangle we talked about in chapter 3 when we were discussing our differences. Because, like with so many other issues of life, at least in our life, it so often comes back to the differences thing. That's what needs the most grace around here. We'll never stop being different; we'll always have our own "love language" distinct from each other's. But we've worked really hard at trying to meet in the middle, or at least to make movement toward it, toward the center—where we're becoming somewhat more alike, despite being so *not* alike.

Mary Beth: For instance, when we built this house, one of the things I pushed for, in the master bathroom, was that I got my own vanity and my own sink. Because if you were to go right now and pull open the drawers on his side, the number of empty tubes of toothpaste and used-up deodorant sticks that you'd find in there (and *I know*, because I looked recently), it's—it's a lot of things.

Steven: Now wait, I threw a tube of toothpaste away just this morning.

Mary Beth: Well, all I know is, my countertop may look a little crazy and messy because we're always going and coming, going and coming, but down inside the drawers of my vanity, underneath, where you can't see? They're pretty. They are *pretty*. And I promise you there's only one tube of toothpaste in there. The one I'm currently using.

But hear me say, I've watched him clean things lately, and he can do it. He's learning to do it. Like, we cleaned the laundry room yesterday. He was my helper. And I realize, if he'd been cleaning it all by himself, he would've gotten through it a whole lot quicker. There would've been parts of it where, if not for my eye, if not for my presence, he would've looked at it and said, "That'll do." You know, "Good enough." But as we worked together on it, and I do appreciate the help, he hung in there and did a pretty good job.

Steven: Right, because I've *learned*. I *have*. I surprise myself sometimes, the things I find myself doing, where I think, *This is not how I*

> *would EVER have done this, once upon a time, before I was "properly trained."*
>
> Like, I think I've already said this, but—in case you missed it, this would be another point-scoring opportunity for me—I make the bed every day. I'm sure I don't perform it up to codes, but I do pull the covers up, and I turn them down a fold, I put our pillows up there real nice, and then I fluff them just a touch. And, sweetheart, I don't know if you do that, when I'm not here.
>
> **Mary Beth:** I *used* to do it. Every day. Perfectly. But he may have caught me on this, because—and some of it may relate to the ADHD that I've developed from having trauma brain—but I'm not as demanding on that kind of thing as I used to be. Everything inside me still *wants* to be extraneat and über organized, but I surprise myself too, when I realize I'm not so hot on the trail of it anymore.

And, we guess you could call some of what we're describing here *grace*. We've found some patches of common ground. We've bent some of our biases around that triangle. And in its own little way, it's been pretty epic, the amount of positive impact it's made. The benefit that grace has brought to our relationship has been out of proportion to the relatively small size of the work and effort involved.

But that's kind of grace's way. It's tiny but mighty—"tiny" compared to the grace we've all received from God and yet "mighty" just the same, even in these little winks of everyday life, these tiny moments of consideration for each other. A little grace, when you're as different as we are, makes a huge difference.

We might even hazard to say, when you stack it up against some of the other qualities we've discovered to be nonnegotiables in marriage—things like honesty, trusting in God, not quitting, prioritizing your spouse above all other family and friend relationships—you could make a good case for ranking grace at number one.

> *Grace:* learning to let little things go
>
> *Grace:* not being so quick to take offense
>
> *Grace:* leaving room for apologies and repentance
>
> *Grace:* making it normal to find mercy and forgiveness

Grace is not easy but it is powerful.

Grace can change your life.

People will ask us sometimes, "How did we raise the kind of kids we've got?" And like any parent, hearing that, we're all ears toward anyone who wants to tell us something they've found impressive in our children. *Tell me more.* But as nice as it might be to take credit for the stellar human beings they've become, there's really only one answer: We raised them to value grace.

And most of it, honestly, came from exposing them to so much of the dysfunction and the disagreements that just came busting out of our marriage. We can't begin to count for you how many times we had to say to them, "Guys, we know you heard us yelling and screaming. We are so sorry about that. We don't want to do that or be like that, especially in front of you. But, since you heard us saying those things, you also need to hear us saying this:

"Sweetheart, will you forgive me?"

"Yes, will you forgive *me*?"

We honestly tried, as much as possible, to model for them the fact that we weren't perfect, that we needed help, that we were weak and needed Jesus, that no one ever outgrows what the cross is made to do in our hearts, and that the only way to make things better is to make up.

The same thing went also for their relationships as siblings. Forgiveness was a rule of the house. If they'd been fighting, we would chase them down: "Emily, apologize to your brothers." "Boys, apologize to your sister." Even if just the two guys were the ones who'd been getting into something, we'd make them hug and apologize and promise to forgive. *Hug him?* "Yes, hug him. And kiss him." *KISS him? No! Eww!* "Yes, kiss him. And then we're going to pray together."

They *had* to be able to admit when they were wrong, just like we did. They *had* to be willing to forgive, just like we did. They *had* to give up their right to be right, the same way we were trying our best to do it. And they *had* to stay teachable, stay responsive, stay humble. Because God, as the Bible says, "gives grace to the humble" (James 4:6).

Grace was our go-to.

We're still convinced it's at the crux of character-building. It did a much better job than all the rules did.

And while we won't bore you with every admirable thing we've heard people say they see in our kids, the thing that we as their parents are maybe the proudest of seeing in them is how they give and receive grace. The Lord has built it into their beings. They don't just believe it; they do it. Again, they've had a lot of experience watching God's grace redeem the brokenness and the woundedness that's passed through our home, but we are grateful to see the same redemptive grace at work in their homes and in their lives today. They are big sinners, for sure, just like their mom and dad. (No, not nearly as bad as their mom and dad.) But whatever growth has occurred from one generation to the next, it's traveled on the broad shoulders of grace. Praise God. Because wherever grace is happening, good things are not too far behind.

This is the reason we were made / to know the love of our Creator / and to give the love He's given us away

from "All About Love"

But enough about our kids. Let's get back to us. It's easy to talk about grace in terms of toiletries and toothpaste, but as we all know, every marriage has much more serious stuff on hand, weighing down the house. Through the years, if you're anything like us, you've responded to some of these heavier things with just about every attitude you can name. Some days with anger; some days with defeat; some days with the wistful belief that things might be getting better. Some days you just try not to think about it. You put your head down, you plow through your have-to-dos, you pretend it's not there.

So, obviously, you have options. Not just in marriage and with parenting but in every area of life. At work, with your in-laws, between neighbors, when interacting online. Whenever these touchpoints start to smell of conflict, when you can feel your emotions getting involved, when a decision is placed in front of you that calls for some sort of action—when it's yours to do, and you can't put it off—what do you do next? What do you come out saying and sounding like?

Do you just pop off with something, not caring if you might be sorry later? (We've done that, for sure.) Or could you already decide ahead of time, whatever the situation, you are determined to lead with grace?

This is one of those moments when we wish you were sitting right here with us, where we could dream with you more specifically about what grace could accomplish in your life, and to share with you more of the examples of what it's accomplished in ours. We think back even to that story we told you about Grandpa Virgil, who most likely lived and died under nothing but the harsh voices of judgment coming from everybody around him. You wonder what might have happened if anyone had sought to do more than just dismiss him as a deadbeat. What might grace have done for a man who was suffering from something he probably didn't understand—the disease of alcoholism—and who just didn't see a way out of it? What if more people had taken time to sit and listen to him? Tried to relate with him? Go to bat for him?

We don't know. Because even when grace is working at full-force power in us, some things in this world, on this side of heaven, can seem unfixable. We can wait a long time, and sometimes we'll never see with our own eyes how God is working all things together for our good and for His glory. So please don't hear us being overly breezy about it, like it's a plug-in problem solver. We've tried hard to be people of grace ourselves, and yet we're still struggling with lots of lingering junk in our relationship that we can't seem to reconcile.

But who knows? The Bible leaves room for "who knows?" Most of us already know what happens when we take a hard line and try to force our will on others. Who knows what might be different if, just for this one time, we didn't? If we led with grace instead?

So let my life become / a testimony of / my Savior's grace and love / this is my heart's cry

from "Heart's Cry"

Chapter 9

It's a Wonder

This whole thing, writing this book, started with us "wondering" how we'd made it this long together, despite all we've been through, despite how hard we've sometimes made things on ourselves.

How did this happen? This forty-year marriage. Is it because we cracked some sort of code? Of course not. What a cocky thing for anyone to say, as if they've figured life out and done it so much better than somebody else. We certainly haven't. Pretty sure we've hammered that notion out of your head by now, if it was ever there to begin with.

But in thinking back through the years, not just about our *own* experience but also about the lives of other people whose marriages and families continue to inspire us, we wondered: *Is there a short list of common traits between them? Do similar themes and priorities show up again and again? Do some of the same threads run through their hands, and maybe, hopefully, through ours too, that we've each held onto across the decades, the same things we've pulled from and tugged on as we've journeyed our way over the mountains and through the valleys that life has taken us across?*

Because if so, we want to identify them and understand them better so we can share them with our kids, with our grandkids, with others, whenever people ask us.

And so, sure enough, as we were talking about it, we hit on some things that seemed to have worked for us. We've tried our best to remember them and tell you about them. And we pray they've sounded helpful to you along the way.

But before we go any further, we want to confirm again that most of what goes for marriage and parenting advice falls under the general category of what's worked for *some* people. And just because something "works" for one person or one couple or one family doesn't mean it's meant to set a new standard for everyone. Just because it's ended up being important to us doesn't necessarily mean it needs to be important to you.

In our case, for example, we're subject to becoming really captivated (and perhaps a little overly envious) reading about families who've moved out to the country, embraced the simple life, organized their daily schedule around the earthy rhythms of the farm, and have ditched the grocery-store granola bars for hot homemade scones, made with milk they brought in yesterday morning from their own dairy cows. Oh, and eggs from their own chickens. I mean, that's a beautiful picture. And we could so wish for it. But here's the Chapman reality: We are the kind of people, whether by natural makeup or just functional necessity, who defy simplicity. We're the ones who too often come screaming in on two wheels, barely getting to wherever we were supposed to be going, and yet—*tada!*—we did it! We somehow stuck the landing.

Well, okay, the truth is, we maybe haven't always stuck the landing. We've had plenty of "crash and burns" as well, which has been the source of a lot of frustration and a lot of shame, mixed in with constant attempts and efforts to try figuring out how to slow it down and do it better. Just ask all of our counselors over the past forty years.

But for reasons only God fully knows, this has been the way our life has "worked." Now maybe the slower, simpler route would've worked too—might even have worked better—if we'd ever been able to figure it out. We're genuinely glad people have found health and wholeness in it. We've craved it and dreamed of it sometimes ourselves. But that's not to say it's for everyone.

Some things, however, *are*.

And that's what struck us so hard when we were putting together the previous chapter on grace, because we realized in writing it, we were no longer talking about suggestions anymore. You go do it your way, and we'll go do it our way, and that's fine. But none of us do it well in *any* way if we think we can do it without grace. Grace isn't a preference. Grace isn't an optional side item. Grace isn't merely one of the available words to select from, on the drop-down menu of marriage. Grace is the save button. Grace is the operating system. Grace is what keeps the lights on and the bills paid, not just at your house but at our house too. At everyone's house. In everyone's life.

Some things are mights; some things are maybes.

But a few things are musts. Like *grace*.

And like *faith*.

When I look in your eyes / I see a million miles across an endless sea / I want to sail the waves and make the great

discovery / and when I hold you in my arms / the beating of your heart is calling out to me / I'm holding a mystery
from "Holding a Mystery"

Doesn't take a genius to tell us our world is in a great big mess of trouble. We've got problems everywhere. Too *many* of them to think we can ever eliminate them all. Too much width and depth and complexity to them, to most of them, to think we can ever solve them to everyone's satisfaction without leaving more problems behind than we started with.

So we all travel around the sun every year, carrying this load of angst with us, because the situation is just so unacceptable. Unsupportable. Eventually unsurvivable. Nobody wants this, this level of suffering and uncertainty—throughout the nation, around the globe, in the faces of little kids, in sudden outbreaks of terror at neighborhood classrooms. Unspeakable things. How many times have even the most well-grounded believers at least entertained the passing thought, *God, how can You be good when so many terrible things are happening here?*

Why, then, do some of us keep believing in Him? In His power? In His goodness? Why do we stay convinced He is not only here—God *with* us—but that He cares? That He not only cares but He has a plan? That He not only has a plan but He is working His plan, and everything He's promised, even though we don't see it all coming together at the moment, is sure to come together in the end? And make sense? And be redemptive?

We believe it by faith.

Faith in who He is. Faith in what He's said in His Word.

Isn't that how we all came to Him in the first place, for salvation? He led us through faith into belief. We trusted what the Bible says about Jesus dying on the cross to rescue us from our sins, and we gave our whole heart to Him. By faith. Because faith is the only way. Faith in God. Faith in the gospel.

Well, faith is what marriage demands of us as well. Faith to keep going. Faith that something better is ahead. Faith that our endurance will not be wasted, that we're investing in a prize, in a jewel, that is greater than everything else. And there's a particular reason we can feel that way, and have faith that way, about marriage: because God has creatively hidden the gospel inside of it. Inside *your* marriage.

Now maybe you already knew this (although we don't mind telling you *we* didn't always know it), but marriage is not just marriage. It's not just what men and women have always been expected to do when they fall in love and decide to make a life of it, as if we humans thought up marriage ourselves. As if it just seemed more convenient to have it than not to have it. That's not how it happened. God created marriage for us Himself in Genesis 2, right there alongside the rest of His new creation. And Ephesians 5 says He did it for a specific yet mysterious purpose.

In marriage, whether we're Christians or not, we actively participate in a human relationship that contains built-in gospel characteristics. Like sacrificial love. Willing surrender. The joining of two hearts into a mystical union, like the way salvation unites us with Jesus—where oneness becomes not only possible but our only real way of experiencing what this relationship is all about. We become "one flesh" with another (Eph. 5:31), connected in a wondrous and mysterious way by an unshakable promise.

"This mystery is profound," the Bible says (Eph. 5:32), the mystery of marriage, because it works within a real-life dynamic that we're personally familiar with—*us*, married—to help put flesh on a spiritual reality that we can only know by faith.

Now that's a lot to take in. That's some skyscraping theology. But think of it this way: *How can I believe Jesus died for me?* Well, it's sort of like how if your wife or husband were in a life-threatening situation, and their only hope at surviving was for you to sacrifice your life for theirs, your first thought would be to do it because that's how much you love them. Jesus died for you because that's how much He loves you. You can see it now because marriage shows it to you.

So let's pull in tight here for a second. Let's leave the world's problems behind us, back there on the evening news, and let's think instead about the problems and issues that are much more personal, the ones you're dealing with at home, in your family, in your marriage. They're not as numerous, of course, as all the wars and wants of the inhabited world, but we still have a whole lot of them, unfortunately. None of them is as complicated as peace in the Middle East, and yet, you know what? In some ways, maybe they are. They've been hanging around unresolved for what seems like forever, and they've proven to be just about as elusive so far.

Why keep trying any more, then? Trying to fight through them. To take another run at them. To not just toss your hands up, declare this marriage a lost cause, and accept defeat, sort of the same way we do when we're bemoaning what's so wrong about society in general, when we've just decided to stop hoping.

What's left to throw at these household frustrations you haven't already tried before?

What about faith? Again, we want to be careful here not to sound flippant or insensitive to the complex realities of some of our marriages, perhaps your marriage, but we want to offer this perspective as encouragement from our own experience.

Because, again, your marriage is not just your marriage. It's got the everlasting gospel written all over it. And so it's infused with God's promises, the same way the gospel is, the same way your hopes of heaven are. You may not be able to see them working right now—God's promises—but they do exist. Promises of perseverance, made possible by His faithfulness. Of redeemed rewards arising out of second chances. Of hope amazingly holding strong through even the worst kinds of adversity. And you can count on them, on these promises, because God also has a plan for the two of you in your marriage. And He is working that plan, even as it passes through these specific problem areas of yours, so that you can discover more about Him, so that you can become more like Him, so that other people can see, in your lives and in your testimony, that the gospel works. It really works. Even when it looks like there's no way it'll *ever* work.

Have you ever thought of your marriage that way?

It must be how *God* wants us thinking about it. Because if He had preferred, He could just as easily have arranged life on earth *without* marriage. But He didn't. He instead put it into motion right off the bat, from the foundation of the world, before sin even entered the world—just like how the gospel entered the world, from the beginning. And it has always been His plan for marriage to mirror that gospel story, in how we love each other and pour our lives out for each other, right here in our homes, right here in our hearts.

And so your marriage is something that *faith* is for. Marriage is a faith exercise—yours is; ours is—a covenant between the two of us, based on the covenant He's made with sinners like us. Because if He can look at any of us—at raunchy sinners, every one of us—and see a future in us worth fighting for, worth giving His everything for, surely we can do the same, with the other sinner in our marriage.

Now listen, if you're sitting there thinking, *Great, real nice, you guys, how you turned this into a Sunday school lesson,* yet you're having a hard time marrying it with the everyday stuff that you are so sick of struggling with at home, we get it. We hear you. When life gets to stinking, it's not enough just to go spraying a bunch of spiritual perfume around. We would never want to do that, to you or to anybody.

We're not pretending we understand all the things you're going through, although we do know a lot about going through things that are tremendously hard to endure or understand. But eventually, trying to understand them isn't as necessary as it seems. Demanding to know the reasons or demanding they go away can sometimes become the god that keeps us from walking forward. If we understood them and could see all of them clearly, if we knew exactly how everything was going to turn out, we wouldn't be living by faith anymore. And faith is one of the things that marriages run on. Without faith, there's no getting through.

Faith in God. Faith in the truth. Faith in one another.

Faith is a must.

Faith joins our hearts to Him / it's not a result of anything we do / but if we are part of Him / there will be reasons to believe it's true / fruit cannot help but grow / if the branch is joined into the tree / and love cannot help but show / in the one who goes where Jesus leads

from "Show Yourselves to Be"

Mary Beth: Routinely when we're conducting interviews at Show Hope, we'll ask people this question: "Who's been one of the major influences in your life?" We asked it of a young woman not too long ago, and I remember she said her granddad was one of them.

That's probably what my answer would be too. I might say my grandmother first because her Christianity had more of that naturally soft and sweet side to it. You had to love the way she lived. But the reason I say my granddad is because he was willing to challenge you about stuff. He made you think.

He was serious about studying his Bible. He knew it frontways, backways, and sideways. He loved the learning of it. Some of my favorite memories of him, as I got older, were from times when I'd pepper him with weird questions just to test him and see him get all indignant about how right he was. And, boy, was he ever sure about what he thought, about his opinions on things. When it came to knowing what he believed, he really worked at it.

Except that I'm afraid he overlooked the *wonder* of it.

I think I can be fair saying that. His faith in God was real, I don't have any doubt. But he was very legalistic in his thinking. His experience of Christian living, the way he did it, was a narrow place where you always had to walk extra careful because God was sure to be out there watching and itching and nitpicking you somewhere. God was heavy on the judgment. Hard to please. Highly punitive.

I'd say to him, "Granddad, I don't see how anyone, even after they've become a Christian, can completely keep from sinning." But he was convinced there was no allowance for it. Or, I guess, no grace for it. "You don't sin anymore, after that, after you're saved," he said. "You just have, uh . . . faults."

Oh-kay.

So imagine a relationship with God that requires not being honest about your heart. Where you feel forced to get good at hiding, at being hypocritical. Where the main reason you cooperate with Him is out of a sense of duty or fear. Where all you expect to hear, even when you're trying your hardest, is criticism. As if God would rather cut you down, or cut you off, than to look at you. Or maybe you just end up walking around with this general feeling that He is always a little disappointed in you and at times is a lot mad at you, like He's carrying around a clipboard with a bit of a scowl on His face. Does that sound like the great gospel plan He'd been saving up for us, all this time?

What about marriage then? What about when we let our experience of it become the furthest thing from what He surely intended for us? Where we keep making it so hard for the other person to measure up. Where we keep being too proud to admit when we've messed up. Where we are so sure of being the only person who's right about everything that it keeps us from listening to what this "one flesh" partner of ours has to offer or contribute.

What do you say we get some "wonder" back into our marriages?

Marriage is hard, really hard, and so it takes *grace*. Marriage stands for something bigger than just the two of us, and so it takes *faith*. Marriage is two people discovering they need each other in ways they don't really want to need each other, or to need anybody. And so it takes *humility*. It takes *patience* and *listening*. It takes *bearing with one another in love*. Like we've said, if there's one Bible verse that's the secret behind our forty-year marriage, it's this one.

And we think it takes at least one more thing, something we've talked about a lot in this book: a big dose of *reality*.

We don't want to hurt, yet life hurts. We don't want to struggle, yet life is a struggle. We don't want to be bored, yet life sometimes is the dull routine of doing the same thing today that we did the day before. We don't want to do what we don't want to do, and we don't like it that other people don't seem to be having to do it, at least from what it looks like on their social media posts.

We want heaven on earth. But—reality check—we will not be having heaven on earth until that glorious day of "a new heaven and a new earth" (Rev. 21:1).

Even Jesus, while He was here, spent only one day experiencing a "heaven on earth" moment, from what we know. The Bible captures the stunning details for us, up on the Mount of Transfiguration. His face and His clothes burned white like sunlight; He had a present-day conversation with Moses and Elijah; a bright cloud descended around Him, and His Father's voice of blessing boomed out from inside of it. Talk about taking your breath away.

His three disciples who were there to witness it couldn't believe what they were seeing and hearing and experiencing. They wanted to stay up there forever, to never leave this place. They felt what Steven's song "The Mountain" says: "I would love to live up on this mountain / and keep the pain of living life so far away." They wanted to get to do what other people only dreamed of, to be the envy of all their friends. Remember how Peter responded? He basically said, "This is awesome! Why don't we set up camp and just stay here!"

But when the moment was over, Jesus exerted some gravitational pull on their high and lofty expectations. Instead of green-lighting their plans for a hilltop retreat center, He trotted them back down the mountain, back into the same old pain and pressures and problems and concerns that had always been part of their lives on ground level.

Again, this old song still speaks to it . . .

You bring me up here on the mountain / for me to rest and learn and grow / I see the truth up on the mountain / and I carry it to the world far below / so as I go down to the valley / knowing that You will go with me / this is my prayer, "Lord, help me to remember what You've shown me / up on the mountain"

from "The Mountain"

Because this earth is where we're made for living, for now—where even *Jesus* lived, when He was living on the earth. The mountaintop has its place. God lets us have a taste of it every now and then—those "pleasant inns"[11] that C. S. Lewis talked about—to whet our appetite for something more, for something that's truly coming to us one of these days. But as Oswald Chambers said, "We are not made for brilliant moments" but to "walk in the light of them in ordinary ways."[12]

To look for heaven in the *real* world.

That's what marriage is made for.

Marriage is an earth thing. People in heaven "neither marry nor are given in marriage" (Luke 20:35). We're kind of sad about that, in a purely selfish way, because for one thing, we can't imagine the thought of not being married to each other forever. But also, after working so hard at our marriage for so long, trying not just to hold it together but to make it be a reflection of God's goodness and beauty in the world, it seems like such a letdown that it'll be over and done with, overnight, in the end. Except that we know *He* knows, much better than we do, how to make us happy ever after.

But what does it mean that marriage, the way we've always known it, is made for this world only? It means, as valuable as it is, marriage is not built to carry all our hopes and dreams. Parts of it, sure, pieces of it, can take us to places of joy and belonging and pleasure and satisfaction that make our hearts feel like they're about to burst, just incapable of holding it all in, this mad onrush of sheer gratitude and excitement. Christmas moments. Grandbaby moments. Beachside moments. Big celebration moments. But most of it, most of our marriage, is spent doing everyday things, running everyday errands, warming up yesterday's leftovers, being just boringly uneventful. Being very un-Disney-like.

And yet that's the wonder of it—that we are *not* dependent on mountaintop moments to keep the excitement level up, to stay content in our relationship, to live and thrive and operate as our best and truest selves. Jesus Himself didn't do it that way. He specialized in bringing wonder into the exhausting every day. And we've been created to do the same thing . . .

to feel the embrace of grace / and cross the
line where real life begins / and know in
your heart / you've found the missing part
from "Heaven in the Real World"

We've got to be willing for our marriages to move to that rhythm, to dance to that beat. Reality is not the opposite of wonder. Reality is simply the context where the wonder happens. Start looking for it, and you might just find it.

And find you've already got enough wonderful here to last a lifetime together.

God, open my eyes and awaken my heart / to trust and believe like I did at the start / when I saw Your hand in every lightning flash / and heard Your footsteps in the rolling thunder / 'cause the sky's still as endless and Your love's still as great / You count every star and You know me by name / with every beat of my heart I can hear You calling, / "Welcome back / welcome back to wonder"

from "Welcome Back to Wonder"

Chapter 10

It's Worth It

If the conditions had been different, we'd have been in our comfortably air-conditioned car, like any other sensible person on a hot, humid, Southern summer afternoon. Our plan was to meet another couple for early dinner at a nearby restaurant, barely a mile away—technically walkable but preferably drivable if you didn't want to work up a good sweat in your nice going-out clothes.

Yet from where we were parked at Nashville's Grand Ole Opry House, after Steven had completed the sound check for a performance later that evening, all we saw were orange cones of construction between ourselves and our destination. So, given our options, we figured we'd probably be time ahead if we just toughed it out and turned what would've been a slow-rolling drive anyway into a sticky but leisurely stroll, going that-away.

And stroll we did, hand in hand, past the guard shack and around to where the sidewalk eventually empties out into this massive parking lot, home to a huge shopping mall and dining complex next door.

But if you twist the combination lock on your memory bank just right—walking through *that* particular parking lot, surrounding *that* particular location—you can take yourself somewhere else. You can close your eyes and transform the hot pavement under your feet into a summer playground—a place where once upon a time people found a lot more to enjoy there than just shoe shopping and people watching and nibbling on free samples from the food court.

And for those ten or fifteen minutes, on an otherwise ordinary Saturday in July, we were back there all over again.

Opryland USA. Ask anyone who spent any part of their lives in the greater Nashville area during the 1970s, '80s, and '90s about their memories of Opryland, and you'll see it immediately in their eyes, the disappointment still fresh on their faces. They are still not over the notion that this nostalgic old theme park is no longer there to visit, that it got plowed under to make room for the draw of national retailers and outlet stores that could drive traffic year-round.

Opryland was a backyard forest of family fun in a much more innocent-feeling time, filled with roller coasters and a petting zoo and carnival rides for the kids. It's hard to remember it all now, but then again, it's really not. In fact, along the far edges of that parking lot, you can still make out the concrete remains of what used to be the banks of the so-called Grizzly River, a scene of imaginary danger around one of the park's splashier water rides.

But for the two of us, when we reminisce about that place and those days, like we did on our little walk that late afternoon, we're not only thinking of all the times when we used to go out there as a family, back when the kids were little. That's part of it.

It brings up an easy smile and a flood of sweet memories, thinking about it. But in a lot of ways, the real magic of that place for us is that it was semiresponsible for putting us together as a couple to begin with. Several important things happened on this now generically paved-over patch of ground that play a role in why we are together today.

Steven: The summer after I graduated high school, my brother Herbie and I landed jobs as singers in one of the music revues that were a major part of the Opryland experience. They were dotted all over the park, with showtimes running all day. Some did Dixieland, some did Broadway tunes, some did retro '50s stuff. Ours did a medley of country music cover hits from across the years, and we did it around the clock. The same ones. The same show. Over and over and over . . .

But I met a guy there in the audience one day who, by a providential turn of events, became instrumental in telling me about the music program at a little place called Anderson College in Indiana and eventually connecting me with a friend of his (somebody named Bill Gaither) who he thought might be interested in publishing some of the Christian songs I'd been writing.

Mary Beth: But though Steven at age eighteen had never heard of Anderson College, it was the only place I'd ever had any real interest in going.

I come from a long line of folks who belonged to the Anderson Church of God denomination, and my best friend and I (a pastor's daughter I'd met as a teenager at church camp) had already agreed to be roommates there.

So that's where I was going to college. I knew it. I just didn't know my future husband was off somewhere in middle Tennessee, singing and clogging his way up there too.

Steven: "Clogging," oh yeah. If you're not familiar with that, it's the foot-stompin' style of country dance I had to learn to do for our show in the park. And I guess, in that way, it was part of our story too. Because if I'd never made it from Kentucky down to where I was singing and clogging at Opryland, I'd never have made it to Anderson, Indiana. And if I'd never made it to Anderson, Indiana, I'd never have met or gone on a date with (or eventually made *out* with!) this brown-eyed vision of beauty that I first saw there, coming out of the school cafeteria, all adorable, all radiant, in her big 1980s hair—the same girl who before long would agree to become my adorably radiant bride. (She usually rolls her eyes when I tell her this, but she's still as beautiful now as then.)

So we had a lot to remember and celebrate while we were taking that slow, steamy jaunt to supper, down memory lane.

Little did we know, however, before the night was over, that we'd have even more new memories to celebrate.

It was only a short walk that night, that July Saturday, but we'd sure had a long walk getting there. This path of ours, the one we've journeyed together, trails all the way back to where we started, back to an autumn wedding more than forty years ago. If the front window of our house was like the front window of some quaint little shop on a small-town Main Street, we could hang up a plaque somewhere that tells people we've been doing business together here at this location, as partners, for a long, long time.

Steven and Mary Beth Chapman
Established 1984

Of course, the cool thing about a line like that, when you see it treated as a selling feature on a company website or something, is that it's one of the few marketing slogans you can't just make up out of thin air. An upstart young business can say a lot of different things when they're trying to get people to pay attention to their products or services. But unless you've truly been doing what you do "since 1984" or something, you cannot put *those* words into your headline. They only work if you've got the years behind you to back them up. There's no substitute for time served.

Steven: "Time served?" Did you mean to say that?

Mary Beth: Maybe. I don't know. Let's just keep going.

Let's just say, twenty years ago, even though we were committed to staying together to the end, no matter what, it was hard imagining we could survive the wear and tear of twenty years more, or that by the time all the damage estimates came in, the battle would've been worth the investment. But that's because, from inside the cement mixer of marriage, you cannot properly gauge the value of what you're creating. During those years when marriage is happening, when it mostly just feels like rocks and sand scraping together, when it's all just heavy and messy and hard to work with, you can't know how it feels to wake up one day and smile to see your forty-year-old initials still carved into it. The long years that go together to make a long marriage, even the long years that felt to us like we'd never make it through them, add up to something that just cannot be duplicated.

The easy joys of just walking together on a Saturday night with someone who knows all your same stories, and feels all your same sorrows, and shares all your same memories. It is a treasure. It is a deep and satisfying sense of belonging. It is like the soft fabric of a sweatshirt that's been in your dresser for ages, for as long as you can remember—a feeling of warmth and comfort you cannot buy off the rack. Still being here is a daily little burst of blessing.

And sometimes, on some days, because you're still here to catch them, the blessings have all the ingredients together in one place to just come bursting out all over.

Mary Beth: Truth is, I didn't even really want to be there that night, the night when we ended up walking to dinner, because my head was

> absolutely killing me. Steven was playing the Opry, which he'd done, I don't know, fifty or more times by then, so it wasn't uncommon for me to stay home and just see him when he got back. Besides, the summer Olympics were on, from Paris, and I'd been enjoying them all week. Nothing sounded much more inviting to me that night, and to my aching head, than a settling dose of ibuprofen and a steady diet of women's gymnastics.
>
> But I'd been told a friend of our Show Hope ministry was supposed to be there in attendance that night, and I didn't want to miss seeing them. Plus, I'm always up for going out to eat with our dear friends, the Redmonds, who we knew were going to be there too. So I agreed to go, last minute. But, oh, man—was my head hurting! The last thing I wanted, just being honest, was being anywhere near a loud music concert for two hours.

Yes, even at the Grand Ole Opry.

The Opry, just so you know, is a country music showcase that's been airing weekly on Nashville radio every weekend, uninterrupted for more than one hundred years, first as a Saturday night show, then as Friday *and* Saturday night shows, now even some weeknight shows. Each performance usually features seven or eight live music sets, delivered by various artists—predominantly but not exclusively country. Some of the veteran performers who rotate in and out of the schedule have been singing from that stage for five or six decades or more, while others, like the ones who make debut appearances on the show, are relatively unknown.

> **Steven:** In fact, back when Opryland was going strong, they used to do a matinee version of the Grand Ole Opry on Saturdays, where people who were visiting the park could wander over and be in the audience. And every so often, they'd pick a singer from one of the live-music shows, like the one Herbie and I were in, to come over there, to get to be part of the Opry lineup for that day. Imagine that! To get to sing a song from the Grand Ole Opry stage. Talk about a dream come true.
>
> One day, back when I was singing in the Country Music USA show at the park, I got a phone call inviting me to do just that, to come sing on the stage of the Grand Ole Opry! My task, should I choose to accept it, was to sing the song that was my one shining moment from our revolving music set—the song that was sort of the national anthem, basically, of that era in country music—one of the greatest country songs of all time by one of the greatest singers of all time—the George Jones single, "He Stopped Loving Her Today."
>
> And it would've gone great, with my mom and dad and my grandma and my brother there, if only I'd remembered the words. But when they circled back again to that chorus, where "they placed a wreath upon his door," something placed a brain freeze on my memory

> recall. And for about twenty seconds—which felt like twenty minutes—the house band kept vamping on that single chord. Eventually they were almost shouting the line to me, waiting for the singing "talent" to find his place.
>
> To say it was embarrassing doesn't begin to capture what I felt like in that moment. In fact, my eye is twitching right now just retelling the story!
>
> But through the years, much later, when I started being asked to sing on the Opry again—as a *professional* this time—I would often recount that story for the audience, where I'd blanked out on the words. Then I'd roll into George's song again, as if proving to myself, if to nobody else, "See, I do know the words to 'He Stopped Loving Her Today'!"

The George Jones debacle was a pre-Steven and Mary Beth moment. We hadn't even met each other when it happened. So there's a good chance we weren't talking about *that* memory that night, on our walk across the parking lot to dinner. But unbeknown to us, somebody had dug up a picture of it that week—of me in my George Jones outfit—and had framed it, and was keeping it hidden backstage with them at the Opry House that night, ready to whip it out at an opportune moment.

And to make the two of us *so* glad we'd shown up there together.

To be glad we were *still* together.

Mary Beth: I'd stayed back in the dressing room after Steven left to go do his three-number set. You can see and hear everything better back there anyway, better than from the wings even, because they've got these TV monitors on the wall in the dressing rooms, showing you the live feed.

Besides, Stevey Joy was flying home that night from Germany, where she'd been competing as a representative of the USA coed cheerleading team, and I was eagerly waiting for her phone call to tell me she'd landed and had made it back safely. Plus, my headache. (I'll stop talking about that. I'm sorry. But you know how it is. It makes it where you can't really process.)

Steven: As part of my three songs that night, I'd decided to sing a new one I'd written, called "America the Beautiful," which tied in some new lyrics around the old familiar ones. It was the week of the Olympics, like Mary Beth said, and it wasn't too far removed from the Fourth of July, just a few weeks earlier, so I suppose I'd just been feeling especially patriotic lately. (U-S-A! U-S-A!)

Mary Beth: I guess it was around when he was introducing that song, when Alex, one of Steven's managers, popped his head into the dressing room and said, "Hey, he's doing that new song tonight. It's so good. You should come out and see it." Next thing I know, here came Greg, another member of his management team, saying the same thing, acting like I really needed to get out there. Because it's happening, he said.

"Huh? *What's* happening?" I didn't know. I had no clue what he was getting at. But people obviously thought I needed to come experience it for myself. And to come in a hurry.

Surely it had to be more than just that one song Steve was singing, I thought. But what *was* it?

The Opry, like we said, is a loose collection of country-styled artists. On the call sheet that Saturday night was a rising young singer named Mae Estes and a modern bluegrass sextet called the HillBenders, as well as a famed session player and longtime Nashville insider, the multitalented Charlie McCoy. But in addition, if you'd been there that evening, you could've heard such well-known acts as Vince Gill and Ricky Skaggs—oh, and Jeannie Seely, who made her first Opry appearance in 1966, when the two of us were just preschoolers.

So it's a wide range of people and eras. And a unique assortment of them every night. Thousands of different players have been invited over the years to spend an evening making music for the live audience in attendance and for anyone else listening out there in radio land. But certain of these artists—like Charlie, for instance, and Vince, and Ricky—and Jeannie too (for sixty years, until her death in 2025)—have been selected as official *members* of the Grand Ole Opry.

Opry *members*? What does *that* mean?

Well, there's no written list of criteria for someone to meet before they can become an Opry member. And it's not like they select one every year or that people know to expect the next unveiling on the last Saturday in July, or something like that. The leaders just seem to know when it feels about right to add another member to the roster. But if you've played the Opry a lot of times, to the point where you've become sort of a regular, and if the crowd seems to enjoy having you there, and if the backstage company of artists and players starts thinking of you as part of the family—who knows? They might just decide it's time to add another one. And it might just be you.

Mary Beth: And I'd really been hoping for that, for Steven—to be the first Christian music artist chosen for that honor—because (I'm biased, I know, but) I can't think of any other performer in the history of Christian music whose DNA is more deeply woven into the fabric of the Opry than my husband's is.

Because, well—like singing at Opryland for those two or three years. And performing on the Opry stage as an eighteen-year-old kid (and forgetting the words and everything). He'd been introduced that day in 1982 by Roy Acuff, one of the true members of Opry royalty, sort of the mayor of Opryland. Mr. Acuff literally lived there on the campus. You just can't get any more Opry-country than where Steven had come from, even though the beat of his heart, from the start of his career, was to write and sing Christian music.

Steven: But of course it really goes back to my dad. Because *his* dream, as a kid, was to be a Grand Ole Opry star. He sang and played acoustic guitar in a little folk/bluegrass group, in Paducah, Kentucky. And like most everybody who's really into their own music, he did it because he loved it. But what he would've loved even more, I know, was making his full-time living as a recording artist, just singing and playing and writing music, traveling around. And, for him, there was nowhere he'd rather be doing it than in Nashville at the Opry.

Oh, gosh, I can still remember being out in the car with him and Herbie—little kids on Saturdays—driving back and forth to his music store thirty miles south, down in Mayfield. Dad didn't say much when he was driving. It was usually uncomfortably quiet in the car, from where I sat. He always seemed to be thinking about something—I never knew what it was—and I guess it occupied whatever space was left over for father-and-son chitchat.

But on occasion, on our way home, if the barometric pressure in western Kentucky was in a certain range and was willing to cooperate, he would snap on the radio and break the silence. The static you'd hear was Dad trying to dial in WSM 650 in Nashville, the AM radio voice of the Grand Ole Opry.

And whenever that signal cleared up—when the scratchy interference finally morphed into the down-home sounds of banjos and mandolins and fiddles and country singers, sawing away at their craft—he'd say, "Boys, that's the best music in the world. That's where music was born."

"Son, listen to the jingle and the rumble and the roar / and the footsteps tapping time out on that hallowed wooden floor / there's sweat and tears and laughter here / and there's sweet amazing grace / and a family's love that always brings us home to take our place / in the unbroken circle of / the Grand Ole Opry stage"
from "Grand Ole Opry Stage"

Sometime in the winter of 1992—so, just about seven or eight years into our marriage—we were in New York City for the Grammy Awards. We get it. We know it sounds snazzy and all, like—who can relate to someone whose album gets nominated for a Grammy, who gets to go to Hollywood and New York and places to hang around with the American musical elite? But trust us, even though this was our third trip to the Grammys (in hopes of finally winning one sometime!) we were no less bumpkins there in the big city than when we first fell out of our family trees, back in Springfield and Paducah. We can still remember the stargazing we did, walking around Manhattan, blown away by the familiar TV and music video faces who were passing by us, left and right—none of whom were stargazing at us! Promise you that.

Like Ricky Skaggs, for instance, and his wife, Sharon.

> **Steven:** Now *that* was cool. Meeting Ricky. I was a massive fan of his. He was (and is) a world-class bluegrass player from my home state of Kentucky, and I thought he was awesome. And a Christian!—which made him, like, the coolest thing ever.
>
> Ricky Skaggs, ladies and gentlemen.

And there he was. In the flesh. On a New York street corner. Right in front of us. And when we dared to introduce ourselves, which took a sizable amount of courage we didn't know we had, he amazed us even more by asking if we wanted to have lunch with them. "Us? You mean, right now? Uh . . . sh-*sure*!" Mind officially blown.

On the way, he paused at one of the many delis on Seventh Avenue and started making faces at the guy who was eating lunch on the other side of the window, someone we hoped he recognized. After a second or two of that craziness, Ricky turned to us and, pointing back at the person he'd just been teasing inside, he said, "Do y'all know him?"

"Do we know him? Michael McDonald?! 'Taking It to the Streets'? Yeah, we know who he is, but, I mean, we don't know *KNOW* him."

> **Mary Beth:** Although, from my days in swing chorale at school, I did know all the words to our version of "Listen to the Music," the Doobie Brothers hit, as well as all the dance moves and

> the hand motions we'd been taught as choreography. Because after all, "what the people need is a way to make them smile."

And you should've seen the grins on our faces when Ricky took us inside to meet him. *THE* Michael McDonald. Are you kidding me? That's another fun memory we've enjoyed laughing about through the years.

> **Steven:** I guess that's what made it all the more special, that summer night at the Opry 2024, when my now *longtime* buddy, Ricky Skaggs, came over to me onstage, carrying that framed picture I mentioned earlier, of me in my George Jones getup from the 1980s. (What was *this* all about?)
>
> **Mary Beth:** That was also about the time—while Ricky was showing him that picture—when I made it around to side-stage, where I could stand there and finally see what was "happening." Ricky was saying to Steve, "The reason you need this picture, brother, is because it's going to go great hanging beside the one the cameraman over there is taking right now—the one that's capturing the look on your face when I tell you: 'You're gonna be the next member of the Grand Ole Opry! If you *want* to be."
>
> **Steven:**

Mary Beth: Hello? Steven?

Steven:

Mary Beth: You don't hear my husband speechless very often.

Steven: Total, complete surprise.

Mary Beth: It sure was. And totally worth the splitting headache. (*What* headache.)

We hugged and cried as soon as we found each other offstage. *Big* hugs. *Big* tears. Because, again, it was seriously so much of a surprise. It wasn't the kind of thing you could plan for. I'm sure you can tell from how we've told you the story, there was every bit as good of a chance that we wouldn't have been there together that night at all to enjoy it if God hadn't just orchestrated it that way. (I mean, what a bummer it would've been, if we'd have had to save up our big hugs and big tears until we were both together later at home, or to have to tell it by cell phone on the way.)

And though the official induction wouldn't come around for another couple of months, in November, when our kids and our grandkids and everybody could be there to make it a formal, family celebration, it was kind of cool really, in the moment, that it was just the two of us.

The way we started.

The way it is.

The way we'd been on that sweet walk we'd taken earlier in the evening. The way we spend most of our days now, these days. Just being together. After forty years.

It's worth it.
Oh, man, is it worth it.

Sometimes I try to imagine / me without her / but imagine a world with no blue skies or sunsets to see / or love songs to be heard
from "Forever the Love of My Life"

We realize this moment we've been describing was a little extreme, even for us. Not every day looks or feels like that, of course. Hardly any day does. But the reason we decided to tell it is because sometimes it takes something extreme like this to make a point, to wake us up, to help us grasp the reality of what's "happening" in all of our marriages, in all of our families. And to see what we're liable to miss, if we don't stick together to the end.

Because the truth is, we *all* are living in and marching toward moments that are as deep in joy and meaning as the ones the two of us experienced that night, throughout that season. And we don't want you to miss a single one of them, any more than we want to miss ours.

The big Opry event, the big surprise, the one that caught the gaze of the camera and the spotlights, was not our biggest takeaway from that weekend, not after all the buzz and bustle of congratulations had quieted down, like it always does. The main joy was something so much simpler.

It was the look that passed between us, off in the shadows of the stage, an instant look that had forty years of "just me and you" draped all around it.

It was having the same familiar hands to hold, the same hands we've held for so long, the same weight and feel, the comfortable contours that we could pick out in the dark—because we *have* held them in the dark, and in a million other moments that were so much more ordinary and yet no less special.

It was the hard-fought faithfulness that God has shown to us by keeping us together, so that we could even *be* there to celebrate such an over-the-top achievement, to "taste and see" again "that the LORD is good," and that He never fails to be good (Ps. 34:8).

It was also the parental pride, three months later, when our boys got to perform alongside, when all of our kids and grandkids and other members of our extended family could all mass up together on that stage in one big sing-along of grateful unity.

And it was knowing we could've missed it—we could've forfeited it—if we'd bailed on each other along the way, when the going got so tough.

That's a scary thought, even now, to think about.

Thirty years ago, if we had given up on our marriage, we'd have thought we were escaping something unbearable that we'd started, back when our extreme differences were choking the daylights out of us. But we would actually have only been closing off all the doors, eliminating a whole category of possibilities that would never have been open or available to the two of us and to our family, ever again.

Twenty years ago, we'd have loved the prospect of making the fighting stop by forcing distance between us, by removing the other half of this "one flesh" organism that seemed to be the source of all our conflict. But we would actually have only been dooming ourselves, by distancing ourselves, to a life that routinely dredged up even more conflict. We'd have been inviting the awkward dichotomy of confused feelings and complicated loyalties that would've run through our family for the rest of our lives.

Ten years ago. Even *five years ago*.

It happens. You know it happens.

We know it happens.

In fact, as we've shared before, the song "I Will Be Here" was first born out of the heavy sadness from the divorce of Steven's parents, shortly after we married—which is why it's been such a surprise to us that it would become a celebrated wedding song for so many. (A fact we are so very grateful for!) At the time it was written, it was me, Steven, trying to express to my new wife, when we were still so young and our marriage was so brand new, how determined and committed I was to being sure the same thing would not happen to us—little knowing how many challenges we would face over the years that would make the lyrics of that song feel like dares we didn't know if we could live up to.

And we haven't. Not always. And even when we have, it's been purely by the grace of God. That is *not* just a phrase we toss out there, hoping it sounds spiritual enough for you. As much as two naturally broken and selfish and self-righteous people can mean what those "grace of God" words say, we mean them with that much truth and surrender and intensity.

The grace of God is what's allowed us to stand together at the cribs of all our grandchildren, and it's the grace of God that allows us to sit together in the stands today when they're playing their sports and doing their various events. The grace of God is what made a way for each of us to celebrate our sixtieth birthdays together at the beach, with all our kids and their spouses gathered around us. And it's the grace of God that lets us close out each day lying next to each other, sharing the quiet worship of a prayer, and then waking up together the next day to mercies that are new every morning. Because we sure do need them. Because we've got nothing else.

Nothing.

And yet because of them, because of God's goodness, because our Redeemer is indeed faithful and true, we are still here. And we've *come* here, into your home and into your heart, mainly just to tell you one thing.

It's worth it.

Still being here. It's worth it. You're going to want it. Don't run out on it.

We hope you don't hear us, and haven't heard us, minimizing the problems you're dealing with or pouring salt on wounds that are already exposed to too much guilt and sadness. Please, please, please—that is so not our heart for why we've written this book or why we've said any of the things we've said.

The only reason we're standing here today is because we're standing on the gospel, the gospel that our marriage and your marriage represents. It says the Son died on the cross and He rose from the grave. He came back from a place of deepest darkness. And because He did, the power of His resurrection means He is totally invested in delivering new hope and fresh healing to all of us, in all of our situations.

And so, we say to you, wherever you are, working so hard to live out whatever promises you've made . . .

We know it's crazy,
We know it's complicated,
We know it's a fight,
We know it's a long, long journey.

But it's ultimately one decision,
Fueled by lots and lots of grace,
Of bearing with one another in love,
And holding on hard to the wonder.

Knowing it's worth it.

Being here, *Still Here*, will
always be worth it.

Tomorrow morning if you wake up / and the sun does not appear / I will be here / if in the dark we lose sight of love / hold my hand and have no fear / 'cause I will be here / I will be here when you feel like being quiet / when you need to speak your mind / I will listen / and I will be here / when the laughter turns to crying / through the winning, losing, and trying / we'll be together / 'cause I will be here

Tomorrow morning if you wake up / and the future is unclear / I will be here / as sure as seasons are made for change / our lifetimes are made for years / so I will be here / I will be here / you can cry on my shoulder / when the mirror tells us we're older / I will hold you / and I will be here / to watch you grow in beauty / and tell you all the things you are to me / I will be here

I will be true to the promise I have made / to you and to the one who gave you to me

Just as sure as seasons are made for change / our lifetimes are made for years / so I will be here / we'll be together / I will be here

from "I Will Be Here"

Notes

1. Miroslav Volf, Matthew Croasmun, and Ryan McAnnally-Linz, *Life Worth Living: A Guide to What Matters Most* (The Open Field, 2023).

2. Tim Keller (@timkellernyc), Twitter (now X), December 21, 2019, 7:14 a.m.

3. C. S. Lewis, *The Collected Letters of C. S. Lewis, Vol. III, Narnia, Cambridge and Joy, 1950–1963,* edited by Walter Hooper (HarperSanFrancisco, 2007), 111.

4. Oswald Chambers, *My Utmost for His Highest* (Barbour, 1963), 152.

5. Chambers, *My Utmost for His Highest*, 152.

6. C. S. Lewis, *Mere Christianity* (New York: Macmillan, 1960), 120.

7. Daryl Austin, "Love Hurts: Divorce Rates Remain High in the U.S.," *The Tennessean*, September 29, 2024, 6W.

8. "There's a Wideness in God's Mercy," lyrics by Frederick Fabor written in 1854, public domain.

9. "There's a Wideness in God's Mercy."

10. "There's a Wideness in God's Mercy."

11. C. S. Lewis, *The Problem of Pain* (New York: Macmillan, 1962), 115.

12. Chambers, *My Utmost for His Highest*, 122.

Credits

Page 10: Song lyrics taken from "With Every Little Kiss." Steven Curtis Chapman © 2003 Sparrow Song (BMI) (admin at CapitolCMGPublishing.com); Primary Wave Brian (BMI) (admin by BMG Rights Management). Song included in the album *All About Love.*

Pages 16, 48, 146: Song lyrics taken from "We Will Dance." Steven Curtis Chapman © 2003 Sparrow Song (BMI) (admin at CapitolCMGPublishing.com); Primary Wave Brian (BMI) (admin by BMG Rights Management). Song included in the album *All About Love.*

Page 25: Song lyrics taken from "I'm Alive." Steven Curtis Chapman, Tom Douglas © 2022 Viewfrom22 Music (BMI) (admin at EssentialMusicPublishing.com); Sony Tree Publishing / Tomdouglasmusic (BMI) (admin by Sony Music Publishing). Song included in the album *Still.*

Pages 29, 132: Song lyrics taken from "Love and Learn." Steven Curtis Chapman © 1994 Sparrow Song (BMI) (admin at CapitolCMGPublishing.com); Primary Wave Brian (BMI) (admin by BMG Rights Management). Song included in the album *Heaven in the Real World.*

Pages 32, 118: Song lyrics taken from "Higher Ways." Steven Curtis Chapman, Phil Naish © 1990 Forty Circle Sixty Music (BMI) (admin by Clear Box Rights); Davaub Music (ASCAP) (admin at CapitalCMGPublishing.com). Song included in the album *For the Sake of the Call.*

Pages 38, 136: Song lyrics taken from "How Do I Love Her." Steven Curtis Chapman © 2003 Sparrow Song (BMI) (admin at CapitolCMGPublishing.com); Primary Wave Brian (BMI) (admin by BMG Rights Management). Song included in the album *All About Love.*

Page 44: Song lyrics taken from "Don't Lose Heart." Steven Curtis Chapman, Bryan Fowler, Micah Kuiper © 2022 Viewfrom22 Music (BMI); RELWOF / So Essential Tunes (SESAC); StereoVision Publishing / So Essential Tunes (SESAC) (all admin at EssentialMusicPublishing.com). Song included in the album *Still.*

Page 46: Song lyrics taken from "God Is God." Steven Curtis Chapman © 2001 Sparrow Song (BMI) (admin at CapitolCMGPublishing.com); Primary Wave Brian (BMI) (admin by BMG Rights Management). Song included in the album *Declaration.*

Page 51: Song lyrics taken from "Still." Steven Curtis Chapman, Bryan Fowler, Micah Kuiper © 2022 Viewfrom22 Music (BMI); RELWOF / So Essential Tunes (SESAC); StereoVision Publishing / So Essential Tunes (SESAC) (all admin at EssentialMusicPublishing.com). Song included in the album *Still.*

Page 57, 72: Song lyrics taken from "We Belong Together." Steven Curtis Chapman © 2002 Sparrow Song (BMI) (admin at CapitolCMGPublishing.com); Primary Wave Brian (BMI) (admin by BMG Rights Management). Song included in the album *All About Love.*

Page 68: Song lyrics taken from "Your Side of the World." Steven Curtis Chapman © 2003 Sparrow Song (BMI) (admin at CapitolCMGPublishing.com); Primary Wave Brian (BMI) (admin by BMG Rights Management). Song included in the album *All About Love.*

Pages 74–75: Song lyrics taken from "Dying to Live." Steven Curtis Chapman © 1987 Forty Circle Sixty Music (BMI) (admin by Clear Box Rights). Song included in the album *First Hand.*

Pages 78, 203: Song lyrics taken from "I Will Be Here." Steven Curtis Chapman © 1989 Forty Circle Sixty Music (BMI) (admin by Clear Box Rights). Song included in the album *More to This Life.*

Page 88: Song lyrics taken from "Love Now." Steven Curtis Chapman, Mary Beth Chapman, Bryan Fowler, Micah Kuiper © 2022 Viewfrom22 Music (BMI); MBSEE Songs (BMI) (admin by Wixen Music Publishing); RELWOF / So Essential Tunes (SESAC); StereoVision Publishing / So Essential Tunes (SESAC) (admin at EssentialMusicPublishing.com). Song included in the album *Still.*

Pages 96–97, 101, 107: Song lyrics taken from "Together." Steven Curtis Chapman © 2013 One Blue Petal Music / Primary Wave Brian (BMI) (admin by BMG Rights Management). Song included in the album *The Glorious Unfolding.*

Pages 104: Song lyrics taken from "Warrior." Steven Curtis Chapman © 2015 Chappy Campers Music (BMI) (admin by BMG Rights Management). Song included on the soundtrack of the movie *War Room.*

Page 111: Song lyrics taken from "The Great Adventure." Steven Curtis Chapman, Geoff Moore © 1992 Sparrow Song (BMI) (admin at CapitolCMGPublishing.com) / Primary Wave Brian (BMI) (admin by BMG Rights Management); Songs on the Forefront (SESAC) (admin at CapitalCMGPublishing.com). Song included in the album *The Great Adventure.*

Page 116: Song lyrics taken from "Take Another Step." Steven Curtis Chapman © 2013 One Blue Petal Music / Primary Wave Brian (BMI) (admin by BMG Rights Management). Song included in the album *The Glorious Unfolding.*

Page 125: Song lyrics taken from "Things Are Not as They Appear." Steven Curtis Chapman © 2022 Chappy Campers Music (BMI) (admin by BMG Rights Management).

Page 128: Song lyrics taken from "All Things New." Steven Curtis Chapman © 2004 Sparrow Song (BMI) (admin at CapitolCMGPublishing.com); Primary Wave Brian (BMI) (admin by BMG Rights Management). Song included in the album *All Things New.*

Page 132: Song lyrics taken from "You've Got Me." Steven Curtis Chapman © 2003 Sparrow Song (BMI) (admin at CapitolCMGPublishing.com); Primary Wave Brian (BMI) (admin by BMG Rights Management). Song included in the album *All About Love.*

Page 142: Song lyrics taken from "Go There with You." Steven Curtis Chapman © 1992 Sparrow Song (BMI) (admin at CapitolCMGPublishing.com); Primary Wave Brian (BMI) (admin by BMG Rights Management). Song included in the album *The Great Adventure.*

Page 151: Song lyrics taken from "Love Take Me Over." Steven Curtis Chapman © 2013 One Blue Petal Music / Primary Wave Brian (BMI) (admin by BMG Rights Management). Song included in the album *The Glorious Unfolding.*

Page 155: Song lyrics taken from "Miracle of Mercy." Steven Curtis Chapman © 1994 Sparrow Song (BMI) (admin at CapitolCMGPublishing.com); Primary Wave Brian (BMI) (admin by BMG Rights Management). Song included in the album *Heaven in the Real World.*

Page 161: Song lyrics taken from "All About Love." Steven Curtis Chapman © 2002 Sparrow Song (BMI) (admin at CapitolCMGPublishing.com); Primary Wave Brian (BMI) (admin by BMG Rights Management). Song included in the album *All About Love.*

Page 163: Song lyrics taken from "Heart's Cry." Steven Curtis Chapman, Phil Naish © 1992 Sparrow Song (BMI) (admin at CapitolCMGPublishing.com) / Primary Wave Brian (BMI) (admin by BMG Rights Management); Davaub Music (ASCAP) (admin at CapitalCMGPublishing.com). Song included in the album *The Great Adventure.*

Pages 167–168: Song lyrics taken from "Holding a Mystery." Steven Curtis Chapman © 2003 Sparrow Song (BMI) (admin at CapitolCMGPublishing.com); Primary Wave Brian (BMI) (admin by BMG Rights Management). Song included in the album *All About Love.*

Page 173: Song lyrics taken from "Show Yourselves to Be." Steven Curtis Chapman © 1990 Forty Circle Sixty Music (BMI) (admin by Clear Box Rights). Song included in the album *For the Sake of the Call.*

Page 177: Song lyrics taken from "The Mountain." Steven Curtis Chapman, Geoff Moore © 1994 Sparrow Song (BMI) (admin at CapitolCMGPublishing.com) / Primary Wave Brian (BMI) (admin by BMG Rights Management); Songs on the Forefront (SESAC) (admin at CapitalCMGPublishing.com). Song included in the album *Heaven in the Real World.*

Page 178: Song lyrics taken from "Heaven in the Real World." Steven Curtis Chapman © 1994 Sparrow Song (BMI) (admin at CapitolCMGPublishing.com); Primary Wave Brian (BMI) (admin by BMG Rights Management). Song included in the album *Heaven in the Real World.*

Page 179: Song lyrics taken from "Welcome Back to Wonder." Steven Curtis Chapman, Dave Barnes © 2022 Viewfrom22 Music (BMI) (admin at EssentialMusicPublishing.com); 50 Year Plan / W C Music Corp (ASCAP). Song included in the album *Still.*

Page 194: Song lyrics taken from "Grand Ole Opry Stage." Steven Curtis Chapman © 2025 Chappy Campers Music (BMI) (admin by BMG Rights Management).

Page 198: Song lyrics taken from "Forever the Love of My Life." Steven Curtis Chapman © 2025 Chappy Campers Music (BMI) (admin by BMG Rights Management). This song was released as a digital single only.